Terrorism, Extremism and the Law:

The Online Spaces and Needles in Haystacks

Dr Simon Hale-Ross

For Charlotte and Tristan.

Terrorist attacks have killed many people all over the World, from all corners and walks of life. Some people have been severely wounded, suffering life changing injury. Everyone has at the very least felt the ripple effects of terrorism. But how many of us actually understand the definition of terrorism, and what terrorism is? In the age where words like terrorism or terrorist are widely referenced, do we know what the label means?

We are all subject to some sort of rules-based society, governed by those who represent us, lead us, and act on our behalf. Whatever country, the State has the duty and the obligation, to safeguard and protect our right to life. In response to terrorism, many States have created specialist laws that are aimed at pre-empting an act of terrorism. Employing the risk-management approach to law making has inevitably impacted upon those human rights of freedom, speech, and assembly to name a few.

The question must be asked, are we sleepwalking into an age where the States restrictions put in place, could become somehow worse than the potential terror attacks that they are designed to prevent? Should we all accept such restrictions in favour of collective security? Whilst most will subscribe to the idea that 'the needs of the many outweigh the needs of the few, or the one', it is often a very different story for those who end up being 'the one'.

Table of Contents

Introduction

Terrorism is an extremely complex and multifaceted phenomenon that defies a single, universally accepted definition. However, it generally refers to the use of violence, intimidation, or coercion to achieve political, ideological, religious, or social objectives. Terrorism often targets civilians or non-combatants and seeks to instil fear, disrupt societies, and undermine governments or established systems. Some key characteristics of terrorism include:

1) Violence or Threat of Violence: Terrorism involves the use of violence, or the threat of violence, to achieve its aims. This violence can take various forms, including bombings, shootings, kidnappings, and other acts of intimidation.

2) Political, Ideological, or Religious Motivation: Terrorist acts are often motivated by political, ideological, or religious beliefs. Terrorist groups may seek to challenge or overthrow existing governments, advance specific political agendas, promote religious extremism, or pursue nationalist goals.

3) Targeting of Civilians: Unlike conventional warfare, terrorism deliberately targets civilians or non-combatants. This indiscriminate targeting aims to maximize casualties, create widespread fear and panic, and generate media attention for the terrorists' cause.

4) Symbolic Significance: Terrorist attacks often target symbolic locations, institutions, or individuals to convey a message or make a political statement. These targets may include government buildings, religious sites, transportation hubs, or iconic landmarks.

5) Non-State Actors: While states can engage in acts of terrorism, the term is more commonly associated with non-state actors, such as terrorist organizations, insurgent groups, or lone individuals.

6) Global Reach: Terrorism is a transnational phenomenon that transcends borders and affects societies worldwide. Terrorist groups often operate across multiple countries, exploiting globalization, modern technology, and porous borders to recruit members, raise funds, and plan attacks.

Perceptions of terrorism vary widely depending on political, cultural, and social contexts. What one group considers terrorism, another may view as legitimate resistance or self-defence. As a result, defining terrorism and addressing its root causes presents complex challenges for State policymakers, law enforcement agencies, and the international community.

A Snapshot of Terrorism: Terrorism is not a new phenomenon

The subject of terrorism has, over the past years, become an increasingly popular area of research and academic study, mainly due to State governmental responses following Al Qaeda's attack on the USA in September 2001. Essentially, this exemplifies how politics and political interest shapes research. It is understandable why terrorism has become such a popular topic of recent academic work as P. K. Manning points out here, the Al

Qaeda attack made a distant spectral reality a closer and more threatening idea saying:

'The imagery of terror is media created, since few people actually saw people leaping to their death or the collapse of the Towers. Yet it seems real and is part of a political spectacle. ... While the powerful and immediate imagery of the Twin Towers being hit, the people fleeing, others jumping to certain death from buildings, the exhausted fire-fighters and the Twin Lights monument opened in New York in March 2002 all suggest that what we saw was a reality, a palpable natural event...'.[1]

---

[1] P. K. Manning (2006) *Two case studies of American anti-terrorism*, in J. Wood and B. Dupont (eds) Democracy, Society and the Governance of Security, (Cambridge University Press) p52.

It was a live event that was witnessed by millions around the world on their television screens, and once the aircraft flying into the second of the World Trade Towers was seen by those millions, the horror of a terrorist attack became a reality in the minds of those watching. Added to the shock of the event was the fact that this was the first attack on the mainland of the USA by foreign nationals since the British in 1812, burning down the Whitehouse.[2] Al Qaeda destroyed an equally as important a symbol of the USA, the Twin Tower Blocks of the World Trade Centre, the Pentagon and whether Al Qaeda would have emulated the British in 1812 with the United Airline Flight 93, by destroying the Whitehouse we will never know, but it is believed that was the target of that aircraft.

This was not the first attack on the World Trade Centre. In February 1993 a bomb was detonated in a parking garage beneath Tower One of the World Trade Centre, with the aim of toppling tower one into tower two, releasing toxic gas and achieving a high death rate.[3] It was

---

[2] R. Adkins and L. Adkins (2006) *The War For All The Oceans*, (Lancaster: Little, Brown Book Group) pp386-390.
[3] G. Martin (2006) *Understanding Terrorism: Challenges, Perspectives and Issues* (2nd edition Sage) pp.19-20.

believed that the 1993 attack was also committed by Al Qaeda.[4]

The 2001 attack by Al Qaeda on the USA should not have come as a major surprise. In August 1996 Osama Bin Laden, the then leader of Al Qaeda, declared war on the USA, which would remain in place until the USA had abandoned first the Arabian Peninsula and then the whole Muslim world.[5] Bin Laden saw the stationing of American troops in Saudi Arabia during the 1991 war against Iraq and the American support of Israel as just the latest episodes in a long history of Western humiliations of the Muslim world.[6]

The attacks by Al Qaeda started that year with a bombing of a Yemen hotel that housed American soldiers, then in 1998 with the bombing of two USA embassies in Africa, killing more than two hundred people, and the bombing of the US Navy's warship USS Cole in October 2000 killing seventeen American sailors.[7]

---

[4] *Ibid* at p295.
[5] J. F. Hodge and G. Rose (2001) *How Did This Happen? Terrorism and the New War* (Oxford: Public Affairs Limited) px.
[6] *Ibid*
[7] P. L. Bergen (2001) *Holy War Inc: Inside the Secret World of Osama bin Laden* (London: Weidenfield & Nicolson) p28.

In addition to this, an intelligence file shows that Al Qaeda was also active in Europe when the German counter-terrorist unit in the Bundeskriminalamt (BKA) arrested Al Qaeda suspects, including an English citizen who was preparing to bomb the Christmas fair in Strasbourg in France, in December 2000. The intelligence revealed that Al Qaeda had operative cells located throughout Europe and in a number of small towns in the North Western states of the USA and that they were planning a major attack. The file indicated that Europol, the European Police Force, had informed both the USA's Central Intelligence Agency (CIA) and the Federal Bureau of Investigation (FBI) of this, but both failed to act.[8]

The imagery of that day, along with the pictures of a shocked President George W Bush Jnr, brought terrorism into the psyche of citizens throughout the world, and it has not died out since, as the wars in Iraq and Afghanistan were still ongoing until very recently. Politicians and senior officers in policing agencies still claim that the West

---

[8] U. S. Department of Justice, Office of the Inspector General (2004) *A Review of the FBI's Handling of Intelligence Information Related to the September 11 Attacks* (November), available at https://oig.justice.gov/special/0506/final.pdf [accessed Feburary 2024] p368.

is engaged in a war on terror as counter-terrorist measures are increasingly introduced.[9]

Terrorist campaigns have been carried out for over 150 years. The term terrorism can be traced to the French Revolution period of 1793-1794, where, in a French dictionary, the term was used positively regarding the legitimate response to the state's systematic reign of terror. By the early 19th Century, the term 'terrorism' began to be associated with criminal implications and started to take on a pejorative narrative.[10] Acts of terrorism have been traced back to 1880 with the Russian Narodnaya Volya group, which had its roots in 1878 and fought against the Tsarist regime, which it saw as tyrannical and brutal against the masses in Russia and the Irish Fenian movement in 1880, whose aim was the end of British rule in Ireland.[11]

It was of course, the Irish Fenian movement that brought about the formation of the Special Branch in England in 1883, where its remit was to police and combat

[9] R. A. Wilson (editor) (2005) *Human Rights in the 'War on Terror'*, (2007 reprint, Cambridge University Press) p1.)
[10] W. Laqueur (1987) *The Age of Terrorism* (Boston: Little, Brown and Company) p11.
[11] *Ibid* at pp34-35 for Russia and p74 for Irish Fenian.

the Fenian bombings in London. Arguably, one could go back even further to 1800-1812 with the Luddites in England who destroyed factories, as this was a political and social conflict where factories were seen as places of exploitation, and at stake for the Luddites that they saw the factories as reducing the artisan to a dependent state. They were protecting their way of life as well as their own independent livelihood, as the machines in the factories were a means of oppression on the part of the rich and of corresponding degradation and misery to the poor.[12]

Transnational terrorism can be traced back to 1968, with the Popular Front for the Liberation of Palestine (PFLP) hijacking an El Al Israeli airline aircraft, which was forced to land in Rome. This action was the birth of what would today be termed as international terrorism.[13] In more recent times in Europe, we have seen the activity of the Provisional Irish Republican Army (PIRA) in the war in the North of Ireland, wanting the end of British rule in Ireland, which started in 1969 ending in 1997 (the Troubles), and the Euzkadi ta Azkazatuna (ETA) in Spain,

---

[12] E. P. Thompson (1963) *The Making of the English Working Class* (London: Penguin) pp598-659.
[13] *Ibid* at p77.

where ETA demanded the creation of an independent Basque state with Basque as its official language where its campaign started in earnest in 1975.[14] The activities of Al Qaeda and other Islamist groups are only part of the history of terrorist activity, but what appears to bring them to greater prominence is the imagery of the attacks on the 11th September 2001, which was global in its reporting due to the modern media technology and global in the nature of the attack. A stark reminder that Al Qaeda do not represent one single nation; instead, they claim to represent a global faith, Islam.

There is plenty of academic argumentation here. On the one side, you have those who say there is no 'old and new terrorism' and some who argue to the contrary. Spencer suggests that there is no 'old' and 'new' terrorism.[15] The motivations of terrorists may have changed due to the growth of religious fundamentalism,

---

[14] K. Boyle, T. Hadden and P. Hillyard (1975) *Law and State: The Case of Northern Ireland* (London: Martin, Robertson and Company) p30. See also P. Taylor (1997) *Provos, the IRA and Sinn Fein* (London: Bloomsbury) p363. See also *Supra* as per Laqueur (1987) pp223-327.

[15] A. Spencer (2010) *The 'New Terrorism' Discourse*. In: *The Tabloid Terrorist* (Palgrave Macmillan) p9

but the concept remains the same.[16] The key here is the most important defining characteristic of the new terrorist is religion, or more accurately, their own identifiable take on religion.[17] Gunaratna is a proponent of there being a new terrorism. He says Al Qaeda is an example of this where there Al Qaeda has operationally linked associates in the Muslim world.[18] However, the Provisional IRA (PIRA) also had links in the Roman Catholic world in both Ireland and Britain. PIRA were Catholics, and their safe houses based in England were supplied by English Catholics sympathetic to their cause. Also, as Spencer points out, PIRA had close links and was partly motivated by religion (Catholicism), as were PIRA's opponents, the Ulster Volunteer Force and the Ulster Freedom Fighters, who were predominantly protestant.[19]

---

[16] *Ibid.*

[17] *Ibid.*

[18] R. Gunarathna, (2010) *Yes: al-Qaeda is an example of 'new terrorism'*. In: S. Gottlieb, (ed) *Debating terrorism and counterterrorism* (Washington, DC: CQ Press) pp16–29.

[19] *Supra* as per Spencer (2010) p9.

Chapter One: The Legal Definition of Terrorism

Terrorism is distinct from other forms of criminal activity and aggression due to its indiscriminate killing of innocent civilians, the lack of a personal connection between the victims and perpetrators, and the motivation to gain publicity.[20] In essence, terrorists do not personally know their victims. They are indifferent to their victims' identities, occupations, relationships, or the potential impact on their families. Surviving an attack often means living with severe, life-altering injuries, which terrorists disregard. Their goal is simply to kill and injure as many people as possible in highly populated areas, with publicity as their primary objective. The threat posed by terrorism to national security and public safety in the 21st Century is significant enough to warrant specialized counterterrorism legislation. These laws, developed over time, have consistently expanded the government's

---

[20] *R v F* [2007] EWCA Crim 243, [29]. See also C. H. Simmons and J. R. Mitch (2001) Labelling Public Aggression: When Is It Terrorism? *The Journal of Social Psychology*, 125:2, 245-251, 245.

authority, with the latest focus on electronic communications data surveillance.[21]

This chapter outlines the contemporary understanding of terrorism, emphasizing the need for specialized and permanent counterterrorism laws. UK law enforcement and courts use the legal definition of terrorism to determine if a crime is terrorist-related. This definition legally specifies what actions constitute terrorism and includes an extraterritorial provision, reflecting the international nature of the threat. By examining key cases, this book reveals several shortcomings in the UK's legal definition of terrorism, such as the lack of precise definitions for certain terms, leading to flexible judicial interpretation. These undefined terms have also resulted in relatively low thresholds, expanding the scope of 'terrorism' beyond international standards. The book then explores the implications of this legislative ambiguity for the rule of law. Alternative phrases to those currently used in the UK are analyzed, with a suggestion that harmonization with international

---

[21] D. Anderson (2014) The Terrorism Acts in 2013, London: The Stationary Office p.84.

law may lead to a more comprehensive understanding of terrorism and a fairer legal framework.[22]

The aim of this chapter is not to provide an exhaustive exploration of the historical evolution of the term 'terrorism', as this would be unproductive. However, it is worth noting that the term originates from an old Latin phrase and was once used positively during the French Revolution but has since become a pejorative term. Terrorism is, fundamentally, a tactic. This book focuses on the legal definition of terrorism. The inconsistencies identified herein can be attributed to a legislative failure, as the political value of terrorism often takes precedence over its legal definition. It is acknowledged that it is not feasible to entirely eliminate this political value, as terrorism is inherently a political crime. Therefore, this book advocates for a permanent definition of terrorism that is as free as possible from political and ambiguous

---

[22] Legal terms must be clear and precise, analysis drawn from Lord Carlile of Berriew Q.C. (2007) Independent Reviewer of Terrorism Legislation, The Definition of Terrorism, March 2007, CM7052, p.21.

language, focusing on its wrongful nature in accordance with international law.

What does terrorism look like and does the UK have specialist laws?

Before considering the law in this area, it is helpful to explore the concept of terrorism briefly and to understand the need for specialist legislation. After all, terrorism is a unique form of criminality.

Case Study

The year is 2005. At 4 am (BST), Tanweer, Khan and Hussain leave Leeds in the UK, in a rented car bound for the train station in Luton. They meet with one other, Germaine Lindsay and board a train to London, UK. At 08:23 am, they all arrive at Kings Cross Station together. Tanweer, Khan and Lindsay enter the London Underground to board a subway train. At precisely 08:49 am, during rush hour and surrounded by many innocent passengers, they each detonate their bombs. One at Aldgate, at Edgeware Road and Russell Square. Then, some minutes later, at 09:47 am, the youngest of the crew, Hussain triggered his bomb whilst on a double-decker bus. Since then, we have heard inquest testimony from survivors, including Daniel Biddle, who was running late for work, still had a 20p coin lodged in his thigh bone, and had to have surgery to remove his house keys and other shrapnel from his body. He was initially blown from the carriage and lost both his lower legs, left eye and spleen. Daniel was simply going about his business, running late for work, worrying about what the day would bring. Other similar stories tell of limbs being lost, eyes and organs, all innocent civilians. But the four men cared not who these people were. The sheer impact of this successful attack cannot be understated.

A catalyst for change

This attack was the largest catalyst for a changed counterterrorism policing strategy in the UK. Terrorism frequently leads to the indiscriminate killing of innocent civilians and non-combatants, posing a growing challenge for law enforcement. Terrorists' abilities have significantly expanded, especially in the digital era, enabling them to evade detection by policing and security agencies until the time of the attack.[23] This situation partly justifies the need for specialized legislative powers.[24] Professor Paul Wilkinson defines terrorism as:

...coercive intimidation or, more fully as, the systematic use of murder, injury, and destruction or threat of same to create a climate of terror, to publicize a cause, and to coerce a wider target into submitting to its aims.[25]

It is evident that terrorism relies on being noticed; without this attention, terrorism would not be effective.[26] Simply committing acts of violence does not constitute a successful terrorist act. The actions that are labelled as terrorism are deliberate and intended to create fear and terror. Still, without horrified witnesses, they would be as

---

[23] J. Klausen (2009) British Counter-Terrorism After 7/7: Adapting Community Policing to the Fight Against Domestic Terrorism *Journal of Ethnic and Migration Studies*, Vol. 35, No. 3, March, 403-420, 404. See also *Supra* as per The RT Hon Lord Lloyd of Berwick (1996) paragraph 1.7.

[24] *Supra* as per D. Anderson (2014) p.84.

[25] P. Wilkinson (2006) *Terrorism versus Democracy: The Liberal State Response* (2nd Edition, Routledge,) pp.20-21. Professor Paul Wilkinson is the former chairman of the Centre for the Study of Terrorism and Political Violence at St Andrews University.

[26] *Ibid.*

meaningless as a play without an audience.[27] For Wilkinson, the general public understanding of terrorism in the 21st Century includes bombing campaigns, shootings and hostage takings, hijackings and threats of carrying out these actions aimed at the civilian population.[28] Conceptually and empirically, terrorism can be distinguished from other violent crimes by the following characteristics such as:

- Premeditated and designed to create a climate of extreme fear;

- Directed at a wider target than the immediate victims;

- Inherently involves attacks on random or symbolic targets, including civilians;

- Considered by the society in which it occurs as 'extra-normal', that is, in the literal sense that it violates the norms regulating disputes, protest and dissent;

---

[27] M. Juergensmeyer (2000) Terror in the Mind of God: The Global Rise of Religious Violence (University of California Press) p.139.

[28] *Supra* as per P. Wilkinson (2006) p.1.

- Used primarily, though not exclusively, to influence the political behaviour of governments, communities or specific social groups.[29]

This is where we turn our gaze to this special relationship between victim and perpetrator. Terrorism differs from traditional violent criminal behaviour because it targets a broader audience beyond the immediate victims. In typical violent crimes, the perpetrator knows the victim and directs the aggression solely at that individual. Hacker acknowledges this distinction, describing the terrorist relationship as 'triadic', extending beyond the immediate victims to include other observers and the media. In contrast, traditional criminal activity is 'dyadic' involving only the attacker and the victim, with aggression limited to this interaction.[30] Instilling fear in the population is a crucial aspect of a terrorist attack's success. By aiming to create fear within communities and

[29] *Ibid.*
[30] F. J. Hacker (1980) Terror and Terrorism: Modern growth industry and mass entertainment, *Studies in Conflict and Terrorism*, 4, 143-159. See also C. H. Simmons and J. R. Mitch (2001) Labelling Public Aggression: When Is It Terrorism? *The Journal of Social Psychology*, 125:2, 245-251, 246.

undermine democracy, terrorists threats and attacks compel states to take legislative action. This pressure leads to the provision of additional powers to law enforcement agencies, with the aim of preventing and pre-empting further attacks. Former British Home Secretary Jack Straw acknowledged this in 1999, explaining to the UK Parliament why special powers and restrictions were necessary, stating:

'Terrorism differs from crime motivated solely by greed in that it is directed at undermining the foundations of government'.[31]

Pre-dating this statement of course would be the then Pime Minister Margaret Thatcher, who when responding to various attacks carried out by the Irish Republican Army in the 1980s and to the Maze Prison hunger strikes, saying, 'Crime is crime is crime. It is not political'.[32]

Jack Straw's statement underscores the reasoning behind the enactment of the Terrorism Act 2000,

---

[31] Jack Straw MP, the then Home Secretary, The Terrorism Bill, Second Reading HC 14 December 1999, col 152.
[32] K. Connolly (2013) Thatcher's Tenure Shaped by Ireland, BBC News, available at https://www.bbc.co.uk/news/uk-northern-ireland-11598877 accessed 15 February 2024.

highlighting the threat terrorism poses to democracy.[33] It reveals the inadequacy of existing criminal law, indicating the necessity of introducing specialized terrorist offenses, particularly given the international nature of terrorism and the UK's obligations under international law.[34]

The UK Government's former independent reviewer of anti-terrorism legislation, Lord David Anderson of Ipswich KBE KC, supports this contradictory view that terrorist violence is not necessarily worse than ordinary crime, and, therefore, recommended a review of criminal law specifically in the area of national security. He believed this should be focused primarily on the necessary extent of supplementing ordinary rules and procedures.[35] He supported this stance due to the extensive counterterrorism legislation aimed at early intervention designed to prevent the worst-case scenario. This is crucial because the current law criminalizes actions such as

---

[33] C. Walker (2009) *Blackstone's Guide to The Anti-Terrorism Legislation*, (2nd Edition, Oxford University Press) p.10.

[34] *Supra* as per The RT Hon Lord Lloyd of Berwick (1996) Chapter 2 paragraph 2.2 and 2.3.

[35] *Supra* as per D. Anderson (2014) p.83.

encouraging terrorism, expressing support for a banned
organization's cause, and disseminating what is considered
terrorist material, all through the use of electronic
communications data surveillance.[36] These actions would
not have constituted prosecutable offenses under ordinary
criminal law, which typically requires a higher threshold
for an attempt, where the suspect must have only the
actual crime left to commit.[37] For McKeever, that action
captured by counterterrorism laws is significantly below
the standard required by ordinary UK criminal law,
whereby 'only that action which goes beyond mere
preparation for the commission of the offence, is
criminalized as an attempt'.[38] The legal and culpable
threshold for an attempt is extremely high, where the
suspect must only have the actual crime left to commit.[39]
Considering the potentially catastrophic consequences of
a successful terrorist attack, law enforcement and the
courts must have the ability to intervene before such an

---

[36] Terrorism Act 2006, ss1-3. And the Counter Terrorism
and Border Security Act 2019, s1.

[37] Terrorism Act 2006, ss1, 2.

[38] *Supra* as per D. McKeever (2010) 119.

[39] Criminal Attempts Act 1981 s 4(3).

event occurs. Waiting until the suspect is on the verge of committing the crime, with their finger on the trigger, is not practical. This is why it is suggested that Anderson may be mistaken in asserting that counterterrorism laws should closely align with ordinary criminal law.[40] Regardless of one's stance on this issue, the UK Government has not conducted a review of the law and measures in this regard.

It is extremely important to highlight the serious implications of being suspected and/or convicted and labelled a terrorist. Such labels remain with that person for the rest of their lives, even if they have been found not guilty. The youngest person to be convicted of terrorism-related activity in the UK is 14 years of age. Held culpable for possessing information that might be useful to a person committing or preparing an act of terrorism.[41] The term 'terrorism' has become increasingly pejorative over time, particularly in the 21st Century, where the terrorist label has a dehumanizing effect on the person convicted.

---

[40] *Supra* as per D. Anderson (2014) p.83.
[41] Terrorism Act 2000, ss58, 57.

Even if the defendant is found not guilty, the accused still has to live with the ascribed label.

Case Study Two

A UK case study from 2020 sets the scene: A young boy of 14 years of age, malnourished, living in poverty with his alcoholic and drug-addicted mother, is missing yet another school day. He feels isolated and alone, which has become his norm. His father is absent, but he remembers him to be abusive, both sexually and physically, and generally violent towards him. He starts playing online games during what should be his schooling hours, often playing through out the night. He makes friends online and often joins teams as they play Grand Theft Auto and other online games. After some time, this child of 14 makes a new friend. This friend questions him about his life and experiences, and they find they have shared experiences. What the young boy does not know is that this new friend is, in fact, much older and is a professional at grooming young, vulnerable people. Quickly, this groomer would have realized the child was scoring high on the vulnerability chart.

This new friend introduces the boy to his version of Islam, which is more of an ideology than anything else. They continue to play the game and talk through the chat function, and together, target certain types of people to kill within the game. For the professional manipulative groomer, this would have highlighted the child's susceptibility to suggestion and the gaining of trust. Then he is introduced to Grand Theft Auto for ISIS and starts playing this with his friend, as they sing songs together that his friend has taught him and chat some more. Soon after, he asks his mother to buy him a prayer hat, a mat, and a copy of the Quran, which she does without question. Fast forward a few months, and the young boy starts making short videos glorifying terror and speaking of those who believe and those who do not. His mother can be seen in the background of many of those videos, paying no attention to the boy. He is then radicalized further into attempting to make bombs and attack a group of people. He does this and leaves with his rucksack, at which point his mother finally notices him and calls social services, who call law enforcement. He is arrested and charged under the counterterrorism laws in the UK.

Although found not guilty, this boy remains in the home that he was sent to whilst on trial.[42] It would certainly appear that the ascription of the terrorism label cannot be washed away.

Once a terrorist, always a terrorist

This could be attributed to the inhumane actions carried out by terrorist organizations like al-Qaeda and the Islamic State. Members of these groups are often portrayed in graphic and disturbing media clips released by the group, which depict the beheading of non-combatant civilians and captured combatants. Justice Collins pointed out the pejorative nature of the label in *R (CC) v Commissioner of Police of the Metropolis and another*, stating:

…once a terrorist, always a terrorist whether or not the person in question has renounced his past or circumstances have changed (for example, where the acts of terrorism occurred in a country whose government, perhaps because dictatorial and oppressive, has since been

---

[42] See https://www.bbc.co.uk/news/uk-england-hampshire-54450013 accessed 13 February 2024.

overthrown). Indeed, the terrorist may have become a respected and respectable member or even leader of that country's new government. Nevertheless, he is still a terrorist within the meaning of the [Terrorism Act] 2000.[43]

The development of the Law in the United Kingdom

The first incarnation of counter-terrorism legislation was fashioned in the 1970s and 1980s. This is where we find the then UK's legal definition of terrorism under the Prevention of Terrorism Act 1974 and section 20 of the Prevention of Terrorism (Temporary Provisions) Act 1989 (PTAs). Apart from this definition being temporary and reviewed every two years, the definition of what amounts to an act of terrorism was extremely narrow. Unsurprisingly, of course, given the PTA was limited to the mischief behind the Act, which was to deal with Irish terrorist groups such as the Irish Republican Army (IRA) during the period referred to as the Irish Troubles (1969-1998). The legislators had no intention for it to be used for any other type of terrorist activity, national or

---

[43] [2011] EWHC 3316, [5].

international terror activity, mainly because at the time of drafting the Act it was not recognized as a threat to mainland UK. After the signing of the Good Friday Agreement between the British Government and Irish Republican and Loyalist groups in Belfast in 1998, the UK turned its attention towards international terrorism.

This shift was brought in part by persuasion from the UK's European neighbours. By 1998, political events had moved on within the European Union (EU) of which the UK was then a Member State. The 1992 Treaty of Union (TEU) transformed the EU from being a 'common market' used for free trade as agreed under its founding document, the Treaty of Rome 1957, into a Union that conferred fundamental freedoms for its citizens. The TEU also created the Justice and Home Affairs Council and Commission to deal with criminal matters affecting the EU, along with the Common Foreign Policy Council and Commission.

Since 1999, the Justice and Home Affairs Council and Commission (JHA) have been implementing the principle of mutual recognition in criminal matters. This was aimed at ensuring effective prosecutions by balancing a defendant's rights within an EU-wide harmonization of Member State domestic criminal procedural law, which also included terrorism-related offenses. EU Member States, particularly France, raised concerns about a new threat of international jihadist-based terror activity, partly due to France's connections with its former North African colonies and the immigration of citizens from those countries to France. French officials argued that the threat was not just to individual Member States but potentially to the EU as a whole. This concern was exacerbated by the number of supporters of jihadist causes who were granted asylum by the UK government in the late 1980s and 1990s. At the time their asylum was granted, scrutiny of these jihadist supporters was not as strict, as the UK government's focus was primarily on the threat posed by Irish terrorist groups to the security of the British mainland and in Northern Ireland. As a result, London became a hub for international jihadist causes in conflicts around the world where supporters were openly fundraising for these causes, which resulted in French intelligence giving London the nickname 'Londonistan'.[44] According to Pantucci,

'What appeared at the time to be marginal and irrelevant was, in fact, a very active effort to attract young men and women from the UK's broad base of disaffected and detached Muslim youths to quite a specific globalist Islamist cause, and in some cases to drive them to go and participate in the global jihad'.[45]

At the 1999 Tampere Conference, such potential terrorist threats, along with the problem that serious organized crime posed to the EU Member States, resulted in the Justice and Home Affairs Council creating within the EU an area of citizenship, freedom, security and justice. The UK's 'Inquiry into legislation Against Terrorism' led by the then House of Lords judiciary, recommended the USA's Federal Bureau of Investigation (FBI) definition of terrorism be adopted. The multilateral agreements between the UK and EU Member States

---

[44] R. Pantucci (2010) A Contest to Democracy? How the UK has Responded to the Current Terrorist Threat, *Democratization*, 17(2), 251-271, 253.
[45] *Ibid*

brought about the change of the UK's legal definition of terrorism that took into account France's and Germany's concerns regarding the threat international jihadist groups posed to European Security.

Terrorism Act 2000

The Terrorism Act 2000 now represents the linchpin to the UK's entire and current specialist legislative counter-terrorism framework. It completely redefined in law what actions amount to an act of terrorism and is used by UK law enforcement as well as the courts to determine if the criminal action is terrorist-related.[46] One main

---

[46] It has also been described as a lynch pin in *R v F* [2007] EWCA Crim 243, [962], a corner stone at [963], and central to counterterrorism legislation at [967].

change between the PTAs and the Terrorism Act 2000 is the scope of activity under the definition of what can amount to an act of terrorism. It essentially widened the number of communities or groups in society that could come under the gaze of counter-terrorism law enforcement agencies. This definition has been amended slightly and added to by subsequent terrorism legislation since 2000.

Under section 1 of the Terrorism Act 2000, for an action to be deemed as a terrorist, three collective elements are required: the action or threat of an action, the target, and the causes.[47] The use or threat of action must involve[48] serious violence against a person,[49] serious damage to property,[50] endanger a person's life,[51] create a serious risk to the health and safety of the public or a section of the public,[52] or be designed to interfere with or seriously to disrupt an electronic system seriously.[53] The

---

[47] *Supra* as per D. Anderson (2014) p.75.
[48] Terrorism Act 2000, s 1(1)(a).
[49] *Ibid* s1 (2)(a).
[50] *Ibid* s1 (2)(b).
[51] *Ibid* s1 (2)(c).
[52] *Ibid* s1 (2)(d).
[53] *Ibid* s1 (2)(e).

use or threat must also be designed to influence the government or an international organization[54] or to intimidate the public or section of the public.[55] Interestingly, the second element, however, is expressly made redundant by way of an exclusionary provision applicable when such action or threat of action involves the use of firearms or explosives.[56] In satisfying the causes element, the use or threat must be made for the purpose of advancing a political, religious, racial[57] or ideological cause.[58]

Comparatively, overall, the international perspective is not very different in terms of the words used to define an act of terrorism.[59] Although the international community have not entirely succeeded in defining terrorism, the

---

[54] International organisation was added to section 1 of the Terrorism Act 2000 by an amendment brought in by the Terrorism Act 2006, s 34(a).

[55] Terrorism Act 2000, s1 (1)(b).

[56] *Ibid* s1 (3).

[57] The racial element was added to section 1 of the Terrorism Act 2000 by an amendment brought in by the Counter-Terrorism Act 2008, s 75(1).

[58] Terrorism Act 2000, s 1(1)(c).

[59] *Al-Sirri v Secretary of State for the Home Department (United Nations High Comr for Refugees intervening) DD (Afghanistan) v Same (Same intervening)* [2012] UKSC 54 [25G].

United Nations (UN) Member States have adopted a series of conventions which attempt to define and criminalize terrorist activities.[60] In 1994, the UN General Assembly condemned terrorist acts as:

Criminal acts intended or calculated to provoke a state of terror in the general public, a group of persons or particular persons for political purposes are in any circumstance unjustifiable, whatever the considerations of a political, philosophical, ideological, racial, ethnic, religious or any other nature that may be invoked to justify them.[61]

Similar to the international situation, the UK's legal definition of terrorism is seen as essential in condemning violations of human rights by other citizens and ensuring adequate protection of both the state and its citizens.[62] It is also argued that 'without a definition of terrorism, it is

---

[60] *Supra* as per A. Martyn (2002).

[61] United Nations General Assembly resolution 49/60 (1994) 'Declaration on Measures to Eliminate International Terrorism' A/Res/60/49.

[62] B. Saul (2008) Defining "Terrorism" to Protect Human Rights, *Sydney Law School Legal Studies Research Paper* No. 08-125, p.1. See also, R. Jackson (2008) An Argument for Terrorism, *Perspectives on Terrorism* Vol. 2, No. 2, 1-12, 1.

impossible to formulate or enforce international agreements against terrorism'.[63] This is representative of the fact that terrorism is no longer a local problem, confined to one's own State or country, but an international issue requiring an international unified response. An example of the need to define terrorism in line with other nation-states concerns the extradition of terrorists. For Ganor, extradition for political purposes is often expressly forbidden as per the many bilateral and multilateral agreements. However, this can be achieved for the committing of a crime.[64] Whilst these are important aims, in practical terms, the UK's legal definition does nothing more than to simply clarify what actions and causes must be met for the UK executive to use in determining if an individual's actions amount to terrorism. Should this be satisfied, prosecution for

---

[63] B. Ganor (2002) Defining Terrorism: Is One Man's Terrorist another Man's Freedom Fighter? *Police Practice and Research: An International Journal*, 3:4, 287-304, 300.

[64] B. Ganor, (2014) *Defining Terrorism: Is One Mans Terrorist Another Mans Freedom Fighter?* In D. Lowe, A. Turk, and D. K. Das, *Examining Political Violence: Studies of Terrorism, Counterterrorism and Internal War*, (CRC Press) pp18-19.

offences can be sought, and the judiciary can then use the Act to interpret and determine if the case before them amounts to terrorism.

The Terrorism Act 2000 was enacted specifically to provide some permanence to the counter-terrorism structure and to combat the emerging international Islamist terror threat. This was identified by the research carried out by Lord Lloyd of Berwick, working with an inquiry team. The research found that the threat was directly affecting the UK, given that many Islamist supporters were permitted direct entry into the UK through the means of asylum in the late 1980s and 1990s.[65] As mentioned above, governmental scrutiny of applications was understandably lacking at this time because the UK's primary focus was directed towards Irish-related terrorism.[66] Internationally, it became a well-

---

[65] G. Joffe (2008) The European Union, Democracy and Counter-Terrorism in the Maghreb, *Journal of Common Market Studies* 46(1), 147-171, 155.

[66] R. S. Leiken (2005) Europe's Mujahideen: Where Mass Immigration Meets Global Terrorism, April 2005, *Center for Immigration Studies*, available at http://cis.org/EuropeMujahideen-ImmigrationTerrorism accessed 11th January 2024. See also Legislation Against Terrorism, A

known fact that Islamist supporters were free to fundraise for international terrorist groups and causes openly.[67]

In addition to this emerging threat, the UK and the EU fashioned multilateral agreements in a joint effort to combat it, recognizing an international threat requires an international response and co-operation.[68] Commonwealth countries and the EU have all provided similar definitions of terrorism within their legislative frameworks, highlighting this fact. Canada and Australia, for example, have the same causes, reflecting the international nature and response required to combat terrorist threats. Although the UK's Terrorism Act 2000 is easily understood by policing and security agencies and the executive and, therefore, could be said to serve its purpose well, it has been criticized for being too broad with terms undefined.[69] The words threat and influence

consultation paper (1998) The Stationary Office Cm 4178 at paragraph 4.

[67] *Supra* as per R. Pantucci (2010) 253, and see also *Supra* as per S. Hewitt (2011) p.33.

[68] A. Kaczorowska (2013) *European Union Law* (3rd Edition, Routledge) pp.17-21.

[69] Lord Carlile of Berriew Q.C. (2007) Independent Reviewer of Terrorism Legislation, *The Definition of Terrorism,* March 2007, CM7052, p.22.

and the proliferation of potential causes represent the main contentious issues.

So, what are the Causes?

Starting with the causes, the notion of introducing additional potential causes was proposed by Lord Lloyd in his 1996 report titled 'Inquiry into Legislation Against Terrorism,' which was commissioned by the UK Government at the time.[70] Lloyd and his team were tasked with evaluating the potential types of terrorist threats expected in the future and determining whether permanent counter-terrorism legislation would be necessary. This inquiry followed the potential peace settlement in Northern Ireland at the time. Lloyd's research led him to conclude that as the Northern Ireland-related terror threat decreased, a new emerging international Islamist threat would increase, making the then-legal definition under section 20(1) of the Prevention

---

[70] The RT Hon Lord Lloyd of Berwick (1996) Inquiry into Legislation Against Terrorism, Volume One, The Stationary Office Cm3420, Chapter 5, paragraph 5.21.

of Terrorism (Temporary Provisions) Act 1989 inadequate. This definition read:

…"terrorism" means the use of violence for political ends and includes any use of violence for the purpose of putting the public or any section of the public in fear.[71]

For Lord Lloyd, the existing definition was outdated and temporary, designed solely to address threats related to Northern Ireland. He argued that it would be inadequate if a terrorist act were carried out for a single-issue religious or ideological cause rather than a straightforward political cause, which the UK was accustomed to dealing with.[72] To ensure that the legal definition of terrorism encompassed all terrorist activities, Lloyd recommended the inclusion of social and ideological causes in addition to political causes, drawing inspiration from the USA Federal Bureau of Investigation's definition of terrorism.[73] While the UK

---

[71] Prevention of Terrorism (Temporary Provisions) Act 1989 and the Prevention of Terrorism (Additional Powers) Act 1996.

[72] *Supra* as per The RT Hon Lord Lloyd of Berwick (1996) Chapter 5, paragraph 5.21, and Chapter 6, paragraph 6.13.

[73] *Ibid* at Appendix E Part 1.

Government at the time largely agreed with the report's findings, it declined to adopt the recommendation for the inclusion of a social cause, opting instead for a religious cause due to its potential to capture a broader range of non-terrorist crimes, such as blackmail and extortion.[74] The UK Government's response is perplexing for two reasons. First, it seems to suggest the existence of a generalized terrorist crime despite there being no such specific criminal offense of terrorism. Second, it is unclear why an ideological cause was included if the government believed that a social cause was too broad, as there appears to be little distinction between the two terms. The expanded use of these causes has broadened the definition of terrorism and ultimately cast a wider net, encompassing a broad range of behaviours.

Interestingly, specifying the use or threat of action must be for a political, religious, racial or ideological cause is not entirely unique to the UK. Various Countries within the Commonwealth have, in fact, taken a similar approach. Canada, for example, covers the same causes

---

[74] *Supra* as per Legislation Against Terrorism (1998) 3.16 and 3.17.

apart from racial.[75] Section 83.01(b) of the Canadian Criminal Code defines terrorism as an act or omission, in or outside Canada, that is committed:

(A) in whole or in part for a political, religious or ideological purpose, objective or cause, and

(B) in whole or in part with the intention of intimidating the public, or a segment of the public, with regards to its security, including its economic security, or compelling a person, a government or a domestic or an international organization to do or to refrain from doing any act, whether the public or the person, government or organization is inside or outside Canada, and

(ii) that intentionally

    a.   causes death or serious bodily harm to a person by the use of violence

    b.   endangers a person's life

---

[75] See the Canadian Criminal Code R.S.C.1985, c. C-46, s83.01(1)(a) and (b)(i)(A) and (B). Code can be viewed http://laws-lois.justice.gc.ca/eng/acts/c-46/page-12.html#h-26.

c. causes a serious risk to the health or safety of the public or any segment of the public

d. causes substantial property damage, whether to public or private property, if causing such damage is likely to result in the conduct or harm referred to in any of clauses (A) to (C) or

e. causes serious interference with or serious disruption of an essential service, facility or system, whether public or private, other than as a result of advocacy, protest, dissent or stoppage of work that is not intended to result in conduct referred to in any of clauses (A) to (C) and includes a conspiracy, attempt or threat to commit any such act or omission, or being an accessory after the fact or counselling in relation to any such act or omission, but, for greater certainty, does not include an act or omission that is committed during an armed conflict and that, at the time and in the place of its commission, is in accordance with customary international law or conventional law applicable to the conflict, or the activities undertaken by military forces or a state in the exercise of their official duties, to the extent that other rules of intentional law govern those activities.[76]

A similar definition of terrorism is also seen in Australia, where the Criminal Code 1995 was amended by the Security Legislation Amendment (Terrorism) Act 2002, meaning that action must be taken to advance a political, religious or ideological cause aimed at influencing or intimidating a government, Australian or foreign, or intimidating the public or a section of the public.[77] What is further interesting here is that the EU's approach differs from the UK and other Commonwealth nations insofar as it does not include potential causes in its legal definition of terrorism. Taking inspiration from the United Nations, the EU specify types of actions that must be fulfilled to be determined as a terrorist:

...attacks upon a person's life which may cause death, attacks upon the physical integrity of a person, kidnapping or hostage taking, causing extensive destruction to a

---

[76] Criminal Code R. S. C. 1985 C-46.
[77] Criminal Code 1995, s 100.1(b) and (c)(i) and (c)(ii).

government or public facility, a transport system, an infrastructure facility, including an information system, a fixed platform located on the continental shelf, a public place or private property likely to endanger human life or result in major economic loss, seizure of aircraft, ships or other means of public or goods transport, [the] manufacture, possession, acquisition, transport, supply or use of weapons, explosives or of nuclear, biological or chemical weapons, as well as research into, and development of, biological and chemical weapons, release of dangerous substances, or causing fires, floods or explosions the effect of which is to endanger human life, interfering with or disrupting the supply of water, power or any other fundamental natural resource the effect of which is to endanger human life.[78]

The causes are, however, a 'useful way of categorizing non-state terrorist movements or groups by their political motivation; ethno-nationalist groups, for example, Euzkadi Ta Askatasuna (ETA) in Spain, or ideological

---

[78] See https://www.consilium.europa.eu/en/policies/fight-against-terrorism/ accessed 13 February 2024.

motivation, for example, the Red Brigades in Germany whose aim was of creating a neo-communist state and socio-economic system'.[79] Wilkinson goes somewhat further than the law provides, detailing a more academic typology of terrorism to include five types:

- Nationalist;

- Ideological;

- Religiopolitical;

- Single-issue;

- State-sponsored and state-supported.[80]

How do we know the difference between the causes?

Compounding the issue is the UK Government's failure to provide a clear and specific definition of these new causes. This lack of clarity has a negative impact on the application of the law. Legal discourse, coupled with the critical importance of the rule of law, necessitates clarity and precision to prevent denotations from being

---

[79] *Supra* as per P. Wilkinson (2006) p.4.

[80] P. Wilkinson (2000) Terrorism versus Democracy: The Liberal State Response (London: Frank Cass) pp. 19-21.

used or interpreted interchangeably. This is essential for establishing a safe and secure legal framework.

Cynically, it could be argued the causes were not defined for the very reason that it allows for the interpretation to change over time, allowing law enforcement and the UK courts a good degree of flexibility when applying the law. In either case, legitimate questions regarding the definitive red lines between religious and political, racial and ideological, can therefore be raised.[81] As a direct result, the judiciary, in applying normative rules of statutory interpretation have been afforded the task of providing a definition that for Walker has in turn occasioned malleable application. It would appear dissemination by the courts turns entirely on the practicality and evidence put forward, where the terrorist group is in essence placed into a category dependent upon the predominate cause.[82]

---

[81] Nicholas Ryder (2007) A false sense of security? An analysis of legislative approaches towards the prevention of terrorist finance in the United States and the United Kingdom, *Journal of Business Law*, November, 821-850, 824.

[82] *Supra* as per C. Walker (2009) p.10.

What is a Political Cause?

Despite the assertion by the then Prime Minister Margaret Thatcher above, it well recognized that an example of predominantly political terrorist groups are the various denotations and factions of the Irish Republican Army, who carried out many terrorist attacks in Northern Ireland and on the British mainland during the Irish Troubles (1969-1997). Their aim was, and still is, to have the British Government relinquish their control over the six northern counties to the Dial in Dublin, unifying Ireland's 32 counties. The threat posed by such republican dissident groups remains set at 'severe' in Northern Ireland and 'substantial' for the UK mainland.[83] The political cause element remained dominant during the Irish Troubles, despite recorded religious intolerance and therefore proved adequate within the old definition of terrorism under the PTAs.[84] The UK Parliament has not

---

[83]   https://www.mi5.gov.uk/threat-levels   accessed   14 February 2024

[84] Irish related terror still remains a threat to the UK's mainland, evidenced by the increase in threat level set by the Joint Terrorism Analysis Centre and the Security Service (MI5), from moderate to substantial in February 2024
https://www.gov.uk/terrorism-national-emergency/terrorism-

expressly altered this political meaning under section 1 of the Terrorism Act 2000. As a result, it appears that neither has the judicial approach to the term changed. Therefore, it is somewhat clear that the judiciary could potentially widen the term rendering the additional causes redundant. This would serve to bring the law into line with Ganor's research findings, namely that terrorism is always political regardless of the underlying ideological or religious reasons.[85] Walker labours this point, arguing that the UK definition of terrorism is too broad and should focus on the chief cause of terrorist action, being political.[86] What

---

threat-levels accessed 14 February 2024. See also
http://www.bbc.co.uk/news/uk-36267052 accessed 14 February
2024. See also 'Continuity IRA claims responsibility for Dublin
boxing weigh-in shooting at Regency Hotel' 8 February 2016,
http://www.belfasttelegraph.co.uk/news/republic-of-
ireland/continuity-/-claims-responsibility-for-dublin-boxing-
weighin-shooting-at-regency-hotel-34433366.html accessed 14
February 2024. For IRA/32CSM see
http://www.belfasttelegraph.co.uk/news/republic-of-
ireland/continuity-ira-claims-responsibility-for-dublin-boxing-
weighin-shooting-at-regency-hotel-34433366.html accessed 14
February 2024.

[85] B. Ganor (2014) *Defining Terrorism: Is One Mans
Terrorist Another Mans Freedom Fighter?* In D. Lowe, A. Turk
and D. K. Das, *Examining Political Violence: Studies of
Terrorism, Counterterrorism and Internal War,* (CRC Press) p.12.

[86] *Supra* as per C. Walker (2009) p.10.

comes through clearly is that the goal of terrorism is to effect political change, which an ideological or religious view may underscore.[87] Comay adds some currency to this point, proposing political terrorism is, in fact, always driven by social or ideological ambitions.[88] Ganor has contended the same position where he refers to a statement by Duvall and Stohl in Schmid's book titled Political Terrorism:

Motives are entirely irrelevant to the concept of political terrorism. Most analysts fail to recognize this and, hence, tend to discuss certain motives as logical or necessary aspects of terrorism. But they are not. At best, they are empirical regularities associated with terrorism. More often they simply confuse analyses.[89]

---

[87] *Supra* as per B. Ganor (2014) p.12.

[88] M. Comay (1976) Political Terrorism, *Mental Heath and Society*, 3, 249-261. See also: C. H. Simmons and J. R. Mitch (2001) Labeling Public Aggression: When Is It Terrorism? *The Journal of Social Psychology*, 125:2, 245-251, 246.

[89] A. P. Schmid (1984) Political Terrorism, SWIDOC, Amsterdam and Transaction Books, p.100. See also *Supra* as per B. Ganor (2002) 294.

The concept of the political cause is sufficiently broad. This effectively removes the need for the other causes.[90] What is most interesting here are the academic debates, which of course Lord Lloyd recognized when considering a new legal definition of terrorism. Lloyd considered this and discussed the possibility of retaining the definition under the PTA.[91] Practically, the UK Government's positive response to Lloyd's recommendations illustrated this point, which begs the question as to why other causes were added in the first place:

The Government notes that Irish, domestic, and international terrorist groups are driven by the same desire to achieve political change by violent means.[92]

---

[90] B. Saul (2010) *Defining Terrorism in International Law,* (Oxford University Press) p.45. See also B. Xhelili (2012) Privacy & Terrorism Review: Where have we come in 10 years? *Journal of International Commercial Law and Technology,* 7(2), 121-135, 129.

[91] *Supra* as per The RT Hon Lord Lloyd of Berwick (1996) Chapter 6, paragraph 6.13: Lord Lloyd stated, 'the existing definition in PTA section 20 "the use of violence for political ends…" could be retained, subject to the addition of the word "serious" before "violence", and an amplification of what is meant by "political ends"'.

[92] *Supra* as per Legislation Against Terrorism, A consultation paper (1998) at 3.6.

Put simply, adding more causes into the mix renders the legislation overly complex when it does not need to be. It also means that these terms can be used interchangeably, rending one or more simply redundant, or thrown together in the mix in the interests of fullness. The Irish Troubles could serve as an example here, given that the republican movement was predominantly Roman Catholic, and the loyalist movement was Protestant. Whichever religion one was born into depended then on which movement one followed. Religious intolerance is the elephant in the room. Therefore, the causes that the IRA subscribed to could be political *and* religious, not merely political. One might also argue, given that the republican groups wish for the six northern counties to be returned to Ireland, that a geographical cause be added in the interests of fullness. Anderson suggested that the elements of the cause be 'trimmed' to make the definition more clear and precise.[93] Trimming the causes is not the same as removing the causes altogether. The corollary of this is that it could leave the definition of terrorism even

---

[93] *Supra* as per D. Anderson (2014) p.81.

broader, applicable to almost any given criminal offence, unless the potential terrorist offences are *specifically* outlined, as adopted by the UN and EU.[94] It could be argued, therefore, that the additions of the religious and ideological cause along with the racial cause are unnecessary and problematic since terrorism is always political.[95]

Contrary to this view, the UK is currently faced with a terror threat inspired by, and based upon, an ideological, religious interpretation. Groups such as al-Qaeda and the Islamic State want to alter the cast of the Western world by imposing their religious interpretation and strict Sharia law. This, on the face of it, does not appear entirely political or geographical in nature. It could legitimately be

---

[94] *R v Khawaja* [2006] 214 C.C.C. (3rd) 399. Canadian Criminal Code section 83.01(1)(b)(i)(A): the motive clause defines terrorist activity as 'an act or omission, in or outside Canada, that is committed in whole or in part for a political, religious or ideological purpose, objective or cause'. See also *Supra* as per C. Walker (2009) p.10. See also *Supra* as per D. Anderson (2014) p.81.

[95] *Supra* as per B. Ganor (2014) p.12. See also discussion on religious tolerance and the rule of law in: Lord Bingham (2007) The Rule of Law, *Cambridge Law Journal*, 66(1), 67-85, 82.

argued, therefore, the religious cause element *is* necessary to capture terrorist action taken under such a cause.

What is the difference between Political and Religious Causes?

The UK has a deep-laying history of dealing with politically inspired terrorism. Religiously inspired terrorism is quite a different story since the UK court's approach turns on evidential matters in determining the right cause.[96] It must be remembered that the judiciary can apply no real substantive tests because no definition of the causes exists within the Terrorism Act 2000. This was seen in *R (CC) v Commissioner of Police of the Metropolis and another* where Justice Collins refers to the causes listed under the Terrorism Act 2000.[97] The same can be said of all terrorism cases, where the judiciary illustrates this reliance.[98] In *R v G* and *R v J* the House of Lords (now

---

[96] *A and Others v Secretary of State for the Home Department* [2004] UKHL 56, [199].

[97] [2011] EWHC 3316, [3].

[98] See *Gillan and Quinton v United Kingdom* [2010] 50 E.H.R.R. 45, [28], and *R (on the application of Lord Carlile of Berriew QC and others) v Secretary of State for the Home Department* [2014] UKSC 60, [17], [118].

called the UK Supreme Court) heard evidence that J had
in his possession a digital file containing a document
entitled 'How Can I Train Myself for Jihad', '39 Ways to
Serve and Participate in Jihad', and another called the 'Al
Qaeda Training Manual'.[99]

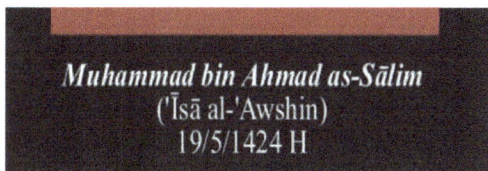

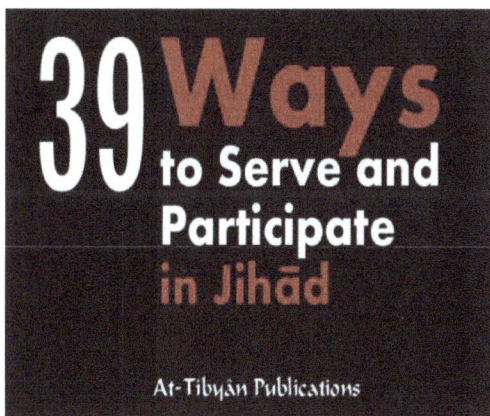

Similarly, in R *v Zafar*, although much more complex,
the fact remained the defendants were charged under
section 57(1) of the Terrorism 2000 Act with possessing

---

[99] [2009] UKHL 13, [26]-[27].

computer disks and hard drives containing extreme political and religious material, which the prosecution alleged 'were part of a settled plan to commit a terrorist act or acts in Pakistan'.[100]

Schmid traces the court's difficulty in assessing whether the terrorist action was inspired by political or religious causes. He argues that,

'...since terrorists generally challenge the monopoly of violence of the state and its ability to protect its citizens', terrorist acts obtain political significance even when the motivation for them is not primarily political but religious.'[101]

Although the UK's Crown Prosecution Service charged *G* and *J*, and *Zafar* with having political and religious motivations, research shows that religious terrorism is inherently different from political.[102] Pantazis and Pemberton argue that terrorism inspired by a religious

---

[100] [2008] 2 WLR 1013.
[101] A. P. Schmid (2004) Frameworks for Conceptualising Terrorism, *Terrorism and Political Violence*, 16:2, 197-221, 200.
[102] A. Richards (2014) Conceptualizing Terrorism, *Studies in Conflict & Terrorism*, 37:3, 213-236, 225.

cause represents new terrorism and, therefore, new challenges, stating:

The *new* terrorism can be differentiated in terms of different actors, motivations, aims, tactics and actions from the *old* twentieth-century concept of terrorism. For instance, the *new* terrorists are inspired by religious extremism and ethnic-separatism (rather than political or ideological causes) and are not predisposed to political negotiation...[103] [My emphasis]

The difference between religious and political causes becomes more palpable when looking at this issue from a wider context. Research shows that in an exclusively religious context, a key feature of religious practices is the ritual of making sacrifices.[104] The impact of this line of reasoning means that the terrorist attack and victimization are often perceived by the terrorist as a *legitimate* sacrifice, in a positive sense, consisting of both attacking innocent

---

[103] C. Pantazis and S. Pemberton (2009) From the "old" to the "new" suspect community: examining the impacts of recent UK counter-terrorist legislation, *British Journal of Criminology*, 49(5), 646-666, 650.
[104] D. Young (1999) *Origins of the Sacred: The Ecstasies of Love and War* (New York: St. Martin's Press) p.208.

citizens viewed as the enemy and the physical act of killing oneself and becoming a martyr.[105] The idea of martyrdom is an interesting one. It has a long history within various religious traditions, including early Christianity. Christ himself was a martyr, as was the founder of the Shii´ Muslim tradition, Husain. The word martyr comes from a Greek term for 'witness', such as a witness to one's faith. In most cases, martyrdom is regarded not only as a testimony to the degree of one's commitment but also as a performance of a religious act, specifically an act of 'self-sacrifice'. The issue at hand is that the terrorist group augments such ideals of sacrifice to fit their purpose. The evil, the killing and maiming of people, and the many human rights violations are rationalized and invoked by a divine law that supersedes man-made laws.[106] The French philosopher Blasé Pascal noted in the 16th Century:

---

[105] M. Juergensmeyer (2000) Terror in the Mind of God: The Global Rise of Religious Violence (University of California Press) p.167.

[106] A. H. Cook and M. O. Lounsbery (2011) Assessing the Risk Posed by Terrorist Groups: Identifying Motivating Factors and Threats, *Terrorism and Political Violence*, 23:5, 711-729, 724. See also Hazel Blears in the Counter-Terrorism and Security Bill, House of Commons 3rd sitting, 16 December 2014, Column 1312-1313.

Men never do evil so openly and contentedly as when they do it from religious conviction.[107]

The UK courts do require substantive evidence to make their judgements. This is where information regarding the group(s) that the defendant is accused of having links with, or having been inspired by, become extremely important. The Islamic State terrorist group highlights the ambiguity inherent with the undefined terms, in assessing whether the group is political or religious.[108] Whilst predominantly religious and following their own extreme interpretation of Islam, the group has evidenced some political aspirations, having proclaimed a

---

[107] R. S. Robins and J. M. Post (1997) *Political Paranoia: The Psychopolitics of Hatred* (New Haven, Yale University Press) p.144.

[108] The so called 'Islamic State' is a Salafi Islamist group following an Islamist Wahhabi and Takfiri doctrine developed historically from Sunni Islam. See G. Kepel (2002) *Jihad: The Trail of Political Islam*, (Harvard University Press) pp.219-222. See also S. G. Jones (2014) A Persistent Threat: The Evolution of al-Qaiada and Other Salafi Jihadists, *RAND National Defense Research Institute* available at https://www.rand.org/content/dam/rand/pubs/research_reports/RR 600/RR637/RAND_RR637.pdf accessed 14 February 2024. See also M. Haider (2013) European Parliament identifies Wahabi and Salafi roots of global terrorism, available at http://www.dawn.com/news/1029713 accessed 8 February 2024.

caliphate in June 2013, crossing the borders of Syria and Iraq.[109] The Islamic State appeared to satisfy the additional factors needed to exist in order to fuse religion with political violence, as laid out by Schmid.[110] Factually, the forming of a caliphate sets them apart from other terrorist groups who have a predominantly religious cause, such as al-Qaeda, Jabhat Fatah al-Sham (formally called al-Nusra and aligned with al-Qaeda), and Al-Shabaab, who follow a similar extreme interpretation of Islam and enforcement of their religious beliefs through the implementation of Sharia Law.[111]

Although the religious cause was added in response to the rise in the international Islamist threat, its inclusion

---

[109] See http://english.al-akhbar.com/node/20378 accessed 8 February 2024.

[110] *Supra* as per A. P. Schmid (2004) 212.

[111] H. Mustapha (2014) The al-Nusra Front: From Formation to Dissension, Policy Analysis Series, *Arab Centre for Research and Policy Studies*, pp.3, 10, 14 and 20. See also: S. J. Schulhofer, T. R. Tyler and A. Z. Huq (2011) American Policing at a Crossroads: Unsustainable Policies and the Procedural Justice Alternative, *Journal of Criminal Law & Criminology*, Vol. 101, No. 2, 335-374, 369. The al-Nusra groups have now changed theor name to al-Sham, for further information see http://edition.cnn.com/2016/08/01/middleeast/al-nusra-rebranding-what-you-need-to-know/ accessed 14 February 2024.

could now be debatable in light of a greater understanding
of the Islamic States ideology, attached firmly to its
extreme interpretation of religious teachings. Taken
together of course with the fact that religion and religious
practices for many is very personal and subjective.[112] UK
MP's Yasmin Qureshi and Dr Lewis made a similar point
during the passing of the Counter-Terrorism and Security
Act 2015.[113] Placing this highly contextual term into a
piece of legislation could perhaps be quite hazardous,
especially when considering the UK Government's aim in
preventing a terrorist attack, and has been seen to damage
community relations within the UK.[114] Since the 1990s, it

---

[112] R. Douglas (2010) Must terrorists act for a cause? The
motivational requirement in definitions of terrorism in the United
Kingdom, Canada, New Zealand and Australia, *Commonwealth
Law Bulletin*, 36:2, 295-312, 303 (3.4). See also M. Elliott (2004)
Parliamentary sovereignty and the new constitutional order:
legislative freedom, political reality and convention, *Legal Studies*
22, 340-376, 322.

[113] Counter-Terrorism and Security Bill, House of
Commons Second Reading, 2 December 2014, Column 253 for Dr
Lewis, and 2 December 2014: Column 262 for Yasmin Qureshi.

[114] Counter-Terrorism and Security Bill, House of
Commons Second Reading, 2 December 2014, Column 263 as per
Jeremy Corbyn MP. See also T. Choudhury and H. Fenwick,
(2011) The impact of counter-terrorism measures on Muslim
communities, *Equality and Human Rights Commission Research
report 72*, Durham University, p.8.

has been somewhat clear that many Muslims perceive that they are treated as a suspect community and targeted by law enforcement agencies due to their religion and those few who commit terrorist actions in the name of Islam.[115] It was the early Prevent strategies under the UK's CONTEST policy that proved most divisive, raising these issues whereby the religious cause element was seen as commensurate with Islamophobia.[116] Non-violent and violent extremism here was linked directly to Islamist ideology.[117] The Muslim community subsequently felt and still feels, to a certain degree in the UK, discriminated against and demonized for the actions of terrorists, using the name of Islam incorrectly, in their view. This, in turn, presents numerus challenges with regard to integration

---

[115] *Ibid.*

[116] D. Batty (2016) Prevent strategy 'sowing mistrust and fear in Muslim communities', The Guardian, 3 February 2016, available at https://www.theguardian.com/uk-news/2016/feb/03/prevent-strategy-sowing-mistrust-fear-muslim-communities accessed 5 December 2024.

[117] See Countering International Terrorism: The United Kingdom's Strategy, HM Government July 2006, Cm 6888 at section 3. Although developed from 2003, the revised version was available from 2006.

and the creation of a British and European identity.[118] Many critics have suggested that this negatively impacts the positive nature of a strong Muslim identity, which offers empowerment and allows them to challenge cultural practices within their own religion.[119] Although politically inspired rather than religiously, for Hillyard, during the Irish Troubles, many Irish Catholics and British-born Catholics of Irish descent felt similarly

---

[118] *Supra* as per T. Choudhury and H. Fenwick, (2011) p.8. Also note despite this point being heavily questioned by the Chair, Keith Vaz, at the recent Home Affairs Select Committee hearing on Countering Extremism, Karim and Dad asserted that IS and other similar groups interpret the Quran into their own perverse ideology. They confirmed this ideology is under no circumstances to be regarded as religious, see Home Affairs Select Committee, Countering Extremism. Evidence heard from Zulfiqar Karim, Bradford Council for Mosques (18 Mosques), and Fazal Dad, Senior Imam, Abu Bakr Mosque, Bradford, 12 January 2016, BBC Parliament Channel viewed 19 February 2016. See also: https://sjiyad.wordpress.com/2014/07/24/7-reasons-why-daesh-are-not-muslim-actually-conflict-with-islam-and-go-against-the-quran/ accessed 8 February 2024.

[119] J. S. Carpenter, M. Levitt and M. Jacobson (2009) Confronting the Ideology of Radical Extremism, *Journal of National Security Law & Policy*, Vol. 3:301-327, 322.

discriminated against by UK counter-terrorism legislation aimed at prevention.[120]

It is essential to note, however, that empirical evidence to support these assertions is light of the ground. Pantazis and Pemberton, in fact, dispute that there is any empirical evidence to suggest that the police and security services are currently targeting individuals based needlessly on their religious identity.[121] In any case, the fact remains that the Islamic State and al-Qaeda do have a religious foundation made up of an extremist ideology. This has, in recent times, been the main terrorist threat, hence why the UK's international terrorist threat level is continually moving from 'substantial' up to 'severe' and, more recently, back down again.

Empirically, figures from 2001 to 2010 highlight there were 237 convictions in the UK for terrorist-related

---

[120] See P. Hillyard (1993) *Suspect Community: People's Experience of the Prevention of Terrorism Act in Britain* (Pluto Press).
[121] C. Pantazis and S. Pemberton (2009) From the "old" to the "new" suspect community: examining the impacts of recent UK counter-terrorist legislation, *British Journal of Criminology*, 49(5), 646-666, 649.

activity, with 87 per cent of these citizens being Muslim.[122]
However, more recent figures show a very different story
(discussed further below) despite the many terror attacks
that took place in the UK in 2017, which resulted in

---

[122] *Supra* as per T. Choudhury and H. Fenwick (2011)
p.75. See also I. Mandoza (2012) What's in a name: Challenging
the word "Islamist", The Chicago Monitor, critical perspectives
on mainstream media, available at
http://chicagomonitor.com/2012/05/whats-in-a-name-challenging-
the-word-islamist/ accessed 9 February 2024. See also P. Beinart
(2015) What Does Obama Really Mean by 'Violent Extremism'?
The Atlantic, available at
http://www.theatlantic.com/international/archive/2015/02/obama-
violent-extremism-radical-islam/385700/ accessed 9 February
2024. See also
https://lawyerssecularsociety.wordpress.com/2015/05/01/is-there-
really-any-difference-between-islam-and-islamism/ for debate on
the terms used, Islam, Islamism, Islamic and Islamist, accessed 9
February 2024.

bridges across London being protected with anti-vehicle bollards.

What is the difference between Religious and Ideological Causes?

Former UK Prime Minister David Cameron frequently stated that the Islamic State group is not based on Islam but on an extremist, Islamist ideology.[123] These

---

[123] O. Crowcroft (2015) What's the correct name for the worlds most dangerous terrorists? International Business Times, available at http://www.ibtimes.co.uk/why-isis-hate-being-called-daesh-whats-correct-name-worlds-most-dangerous-terrorists-1531506 accessed 9 February 2024. See also http://www.dnaindia.com/world/report-isis-is-not-islamic-call-them-daesh-david-cameron-2151363 accessed 9 February 2024.

Islamist groups are based on an extreme view of Sunni Islam, known as Salafi and Wahhabism, upon which the doctrine of Takfir rests. Such a political statement conforms with Neumann's theory surrounding radicalization, which posits that two elements are always present.[124] First, there must be a grievance, usually rooted in political discontent, and, secondly, an ideology.[125] Anderson provided evidence for this, relying on Neumann's theory, where he confirmed that a quarter of all terrorists currently serving custodial sentences in the UK are, in fact, those who had converted (or reverted) to Islam.[126] Perhaps then, they are not practising religious beliefs at all, but rather an ideological belief founded on religion, as suggested by Cameron's assertion. This suggests a greater political understanding of the 21st-

---

[124] P. R. Neumann, opinion cited in M. Sedgwick (2010) The Concept of Radicalisation as a Source of Confusion, *Terrorism and Political Violence*, Vol. 22, No. 4, 480.

[125] A. P. Schmid (2013) Radicalisation, De-Radicalisation, Counter-Radicalisation: A Conceptual Discussion and Literature Review, International Centre for Counter-Terrorism-The Hague (ICCT), p.3.

[126] Home Affairs Select Committee, Countering Extremism. Evidence heard from David Anderson KC, Independent Reviewer of Anti-Terrorism Legislation, 19 January 2016, BBC Parliament Channel viewed 19 February 2024.

century terrorist threat and perhaps a move away from the religious cause element. Emphasis is grounded more firmly, therefore, on the political value of the terrorist label. Rather than having definitive legal definitions for such phrases, politicians can effectively remove all references to either of them or alter the meaning of the phrases to suit their particular needs at any given time, thereby applying them malleably.

Cynically, Pantucci indicates this is the case by putting forward the argument that by adding a religious cause into the UK legal definition of terrorism, the UK Government can effectively decide who are good Muslims and who are bad, by their own engagement within the communities.[127] However, it could be argued that rather than the negative viewpoint put forward here by Pantucci, it represents simply a matter of UK law enforcement and the Government making their way through a new threat that they did not entirely understand. In the early days of the Islamist threat, UK policing and security agencies were

---

[127] R. Pantucci (2010) A contest to democracy? How the UK has responded to the current terrorist threat *Democratization* 17(2), 251-271, 262.

learning about this new threat first-hand. As such, an urgency followed, and serious questions required answering, such as who they were and what type of threat they posed.[128]

The ideological cause, in particular, is perhaps better referred to as a 'catch-all' cause. The problem here is the broadness of the term 'ideological' that could potentially capture anything such as animal rights groups' activity or anti-abortion groups not normally associated with the 21st-century general understanding of terrorism.[129] During the drafting stages of the Terrorism Act 2000, parliamentarians raised concerns about the inclusion of ideological causes. The then Home Secretary Jack Straw was questioned as to whether or not industrial strike action would amount to an act of terrorism, as per the definition, which was topical at the time given the UK firefighters were on a national strike.[130] Such action could

---

[128] See, https://www.mi5.gov.uk/the-rise-of-the-islamist-terrorist-threat and also
https://www.theguardian.com/commentisfree/2016/apr/04/prevent-hate-muslims-schools-terrorism-teachers-reject accessed Feburary 2024.

[129] *Supra* as per P. Wilkinson (2006) p.4.

[130] *Supra* as per C. Walker (2009) at p.10.

have been perceived as influencing the Government for an ideological cause, to alter its policy on pay and working conditions and subsequently found to be endangering people's lives by withdrawing labour.[131]

Although the Home Secretary unequivocally confirmed that industrial action would be omitted from capture, this fact is not reflected in the legislation, despite his assurances the ideological cause was aimed at action by eco-terrorism, anti-abortion groups and animal liberation groups mentioned above. Without legislative certainty, the suggestion is transmitted that there is little in place to stop a successive government from deeming such action as terrorist legitimately. Furthermore, industrial action has been expressly omitted from the legal definition of terrorism in Canada and Australia. In addition to omitting industrial action, the Canadian legal definition of terrorism does not include an act or omission committed during an armed conflict, as in accordance with customary international law, or the activities by military forces or a

---

[131] *Ibid.*

state in the exercise of their duties, as discussed further below.[132]

What about my Freedom of Expression?

When considering further counter-terrorism legislation, the effectiveness of the causes element within the Terrorism Act 2000 are undeniable. Sections 1 and 2 of the Terrorism Act 2006, for example, relying on the causes, created new types of terrorist offences. Enacted in the aftermath of the 7th July London bombings in 2005, the provisions were introduced to deal with religious extremist hate preachers and the enormous amount of extremist religious text available in print and online that served to influence others to become terrorists.

---

[132] *Ibid.*

To this end, section 1 criminalizes the encouragement of terrorism, and Section 2 the distribution of terrorist publications which may inspire terrorist action.[133] In practice, this broadly phrased Act can then be used by policing and security agencies when differentiating between freedom of expression and expression that crosses the line into potential terrorist activity when carrying out electronic communications data surveillance under an Investigatory Powers Act 2016 authority.

Utilizing this authority, if law enforcement, monitoring electronic communications data through the Investigatory Powers Act authority, discovered, for example, a citizen planning to carry out attacks in the name of the Irish republican cause, then this may satisfy the political element. Similarly, suppose a person were to advocate serious violence with the aim of preserving animal rights, perhaps by attempting to force the UK to keep the Hunting Act 2004 in place. In that case, this may

---

[133] These can be committed recklessly, which certainly has an impact on article 10 Freedom of expression under the European Convention of Human Rights.

raise law enforcement's alarm when picking up electronic communications data that could be seen as potentially terrorist acts, satisfying the ideological element.

This is further emphasized by the fact that the provisions in the Terrorism Act 2006 rely on the definition of terrorism under the Terrorism Act 2000, as was raised prior to the enactment in the Third Report of Session 2005–06 of the Joint Committee of the House of Lords and House of Commons on Human Rights.[134] The breadth of the Terrorism Act 2006 mixed together with the broad definition of terrorism raised serious concerns for the Committee where they found 'the creation of the offence of encouragement of terrorism defined as broadly as in section 1 of the Terrorism Act 2000 is to criminalize any expression of a view that armed resistance to a brutal or repressive anti-democratic regime might in certain circumstances be justifiable, even where such resistance consists of campaigns of sabotage against property, and specifically directed away from human casualties'.[135] Former Home Secretary John Reid MP admitted this was

---

[134] HL Paper 75-I, HC 561-I.
[135] *Ibid* at paragraph 12.

the effect of the offence but went on to defend the scope, saying:

…there is nowhere in the world today where violence can be justified as a means of bringing about political change.[136]

The Committee remained concerned and called, therefore, for urgent changes to the definition of terrorism in an effort to constrain it in line with the EU Council Framework Decision and the UN Security Council Resolution 1566. The Committee stated this was necessary 'to avoid a high risk of such provisions being found to be incompatible with Article 10 European Convention on Human freedom of expression and related Articles'.[137] Other low threshold parts to the definition of terrorism were pointed out in this regard, such as the phrase 'influence'.

Parking the scope to one side for a moment, the 2006 Act has not been particularly successful for the UK, given

---

[136] *Ibid.*

[137] *Ibid,* In attempting to satisfy the Committee's concerns, the then Home Secretary announced Lord Carlile or Berriew would undertake a review of the definition of terrorism.

there have only been a few convictions since enactment. This could be due to the high threshold of evidence required and could also be in part because these types of terrorist activities take place on the internet, or more accurately, the Darknet, out of sight of law enforcement and untraceable. Since the Investigatory Powers Act 2016 was passed, the chances afforded to counter-terrorism law enforcement's alarm being raised by such behaviour have increased. They are, in fact, set on the course to increase further by the passing of the Online Safety Act 2023. Testing whether or not the line into terrorist activity has been crossed, the Investigatory Powers Act's bulk interception, bulk acquisition, and bulk equipment interference powers play a huge role in the 21st Century, in the digital age. This, in turn, could generate a surge in the use of the Terrorism Act 2006.

Setting the bar low and casting the net wider than ever, the phrase influence is extraordinarily broad, especially when taken together with the ideological cause. The use of this phrase does not fit comparatively with other jurisdictions, particularly when noting the fact that protests and industrial actions are not expressly safeguarded under UK legislation.[138] Illustrative of the UK's old capability to effectively 'gold-plate' EU law and international law, utilizing catch-all phrasing of this nature is not entirely surprising. It has since been heavily criticized by many, including Lord Anderson, as setting the bar 'remarkably low'.[139] In Anderson's analysis, he draws on comparable definitions from the EU, Council of Europe, the UN, Commonwealth countries and the United States of America, where the standard is set higher. Within their other jurisdictions, the word influence is substituted for the words 'compel,[140] unduly compel,[141]

[138] See the Canadian Criminal Code R.S.C.1985, c. C-46, s83.01(1)(b)(ii)(E).

[139] *Supra* as per D. Anderson (2014) p.85.

[140] Canadian Criminal Code R.S.C.1985, c. C-46.

[141] Council Framework Decision on combating terrorism 2002/475/JHA.

influence by intimidation,[142] coerce,[143] intimidate,[144] and force'.[145] Lord Lloyd, in drawing from the USA Federal Bureau of Investigation's definition, suggested that 'to intimidate or coerce a government' should become the set standard.[146] In attempting to satisfy the concerns raised in the Third Report of Session 2005–06 of the Joint Committee of the House of Lords and House of

---

[142] Uniting and Strengthening America by Providing Appropriate Tools Required to Intercept and Obstruct Terrorism Act of 2001, section 2331, Part 1 Chapter 113B (ii) of the United States Code 18. However, when assessing domestic terrorism the threshold is lowered to 'influence the policy of a government', under Part 5B(ii).

[143] The Federal Bureau of Investigation's US Code of Federal Regulations, see http://www.fbi.gov/about-us/investigate/terrorism/terrorism-definition accessed Feburary 2024.

[144] *Ibid.*

[145] *Supra* as per D. Anderson (2014) p.86.

[146] *Supra* as per The RT Hon Lord Lloyd of Berwick (1996) Appendix E, Part 1. See also G. Joffe (2008) The European Union, Democracy and Counter-Terrorism in the Maghreb, *Journal of Common Market Studies* 46(1), 147-171, 155. The Federal Bureau of Investigation's US Code of Federal Regulations defines terrorism as, '...the unlawful use of force and violence against persons or property to intimidate or coerce a government, the civilian population, or any segment thereof, in furtherance of political or social objectives'. The Federal Bureau of Investigation's US Code of Federal Regulations, see http://www.fbi.gov/about-us/investigate/terrorism/terrorism-definition accessed Feburary 2024.

Commons on Human Rights, the then Home Secretary John Reid MP announced Lord Carlile of Berriew would undertake a review of the definition of terrorism. Carlile inevitably agreed with Lloyd and pressed the point in his 2007 report to the then Government:

The existing law should be amended [to ensure] actions cease to fall within the definition of terrorism if intended *only to influence...* [My emphasis][147]

This, in fact, made very little difference in the end, as John Reid defended the existing law in his reply to Carlile. Here, he explained that he did not see the use of the phrase influence as setting the bar too low. It would appear that despite the reservations over this low threshold, advanced by not only the many independent reviewers but also the judiciary and academic community, the UK government remains unwilling to change it.[148] According to Anderson's findings, the rationale behind the unwillingness to raise the threshold to 'intimidate', for instance, is that the phrase itself removes the possibility of

---

[147] *Supra* as per Lord Carlile of Berriew Q.C. (2007) p.47.

[148] *Supra* as per D. Anderson (2014) p.88.

argumentation being raised surrounding whether or not
the Government can actually be intimidated by terrorist
actions or threat of actions.[149] An example of hostage
taking was posed, whereby the release negotiated by the
Government, or an international organization, would
come more readily within the ambit of influence, rather
than intimidate.[150] Anderson was not swayed by this
argument and, valorizing his position, it is suggested that
the phrase 'unduly compel' should serve as 'influences'
replacement. Considering that influencing the
Government is the legitimate aim of all political activity,
such as the recent strike action by junior doctors in 2016
and 2023/2024, it is arguably unsafe for the UK
Government to continue its use in counter-terrorism
legislation.[151] Regardless, this poses another sub-question
as to whether or not the Government can actually be
intimidated or influenced, or indeed, the life of the nation

---

[149] *Ibid.*

[150] *Ibid.*

[151] P. Crish (2016) Junior doctors' strikes will continue as
minister plans to impose new contracts, CIPD available at:
http://www.cipd.co.uk/pm/peoplemanagement/b/weblog/archive/2
016/02/12/junior-doctors-39-strikes-will-continue-as-minister-
plans-to-impose-new-contracts.aspx accessed 13 February 2024.

threatened by an act of terrorism. This issue was, in fact, raised in *A and Others v Secretary of State for the Home Department,* where Lord Hoffmann made it clear that citizens' lives are incomparable with the life of the nation:

…its institutions and values endure through generations…England is the same nation as it was at the time of the first Elizabeth or the Glorious Revolution. The [Spanish] Armada threatened to destroy the life of the nation, not by loss of life in battle, but by subjecting English institutions to the rule of Spain and the Inquisition. The same was true of the threat posed to the [UK] by Nazi Germany in the Second World War. This country, more than any other in the world, has an unbroken history of living for centuries under institutions and in accordance with values which show a recognizable continuity.[152]

The European Union's approach certainly seems to raise the threshold, where Article 1 of the EU Council

---

[152] *A and Others v Secretary of State for the Home Department* [2004] UKHL 56, [91].

Framework Decision on combating terrorism provides that terrorism includes:

1. Seriously intimidating a population; or

2. Unduly compelling a government or international organization to perform or abstain from performing any act; or

3. Seriously destabilizing or destroying the fundamental political, constitutional, economic or social structures of a country or an international organization.[153]

The actions that amount to terrorism are, in fact, similar to the UK and Commonwealth countries.[154] The phrases used, however, appear to raise the threshold in terms of what *aims* amount to terrorism. As opposed to the UK's 'intimidate the public' and 'influence a government', the EU's model stipulates that the action must 'seriously intimidate a population' and 'unduly compel a government'.[155] This is a much more thorough definition. Noteworthy here is the fact that no counter-

---

[153] *Supra* as per EU Council Framework Decision, (2002/475/JHA).

[154] *Ibid.*

[155] *Ibid.*

terrorism legislation existed in the EU prior to al-Qaeda's terrorist attacks on the 11th September 2001 on the USA. The EU responded to this attack by introducing the framework decision previously mentioned.[156] The purpose was to ensure Member States responded to the transnational threat and to enable co-operation between them supported by EU policy programmes.[157]

The then EU's Justice and Home Affairs Council confirmed that the protection of the lives and property of its citizens', within the area of citizenship, freedom, security and justice, is the core task providing legitimacy to extensive public powers and policies. The expectation here is set, where EU citizens' expect EU action to protect their health and safety.[158] Revisiting the Canadian

---

[156] C. C. Murphy (2015) *EU Counter-Terrorism Law: Pre-Emption and the Rule of Law*, (Oxford: Hart Publishing) p.17.

[157] Commission (EC) (2007) Report from the Commission based on Art 11 of the Council Framework decision of 13 June 2002 on combatting terrorism, Brussels, COM(2007)681 6th November 2007, p.10.

[158] Council of the European Communities (2005) Communication from the Commission to the Council and the European Parliament Brussels COM(2005)124 6th April 2005, p.2. See also Council of the European Union (2005a) The European Union Counter-terrorism Strategy 14469/4/05 30th November 2005.

definition for the moment, section 83.01(1) and (b) of the Canadian Criminal Code defines terrorism as:

...as an act or an omission, inside or outside Canada, that is committed for a political, religious or ideological objective or cause, and with the intention of *intimidating* the public or a segment of the public, or *compelling* a person, government or organization to do or to refrain from doing any act, whether inside or outside of Canada.[159] [My emphasis]

Although the 'compelling' element raises the threshold, the addition of 'person' arguably balances this. The UK specifies that 'serious' violence is required against mere 'violence' here, albeit intentionally:

...causes death or serious bodily harm to a person, endangers a person's life, causes a serious risk to the health or safety of the public or any segment of the public, causes substantial property damage, whether to public or private

---

[159] See the Canadian Criminal Code R.S.C.1985, c. C-46, s83.01(1)(a) and (b)(i)(A) and (B). See also R. Douglas (2010) Must terrorists act for a cause? The motivational requirement in definitions of terrorism in the United Kingdom, Canada, New Zealand and Australia, *Commonwealth Law Bulletin* 36(2), 295-312, 295.

property, if causing such damage is likely to result in the conduct or harm referred to in any of clauses (A) to (C), or, causes serious interference with or serious disruption of an essential service, facility or system, whether public or private, other than as a result of advocacy, protest, dissent or stoppage of work that is not intended to result in conduct referred to in any of clauses (A) to (C).[160]

The Canadian definition explicitly includes:

Conspiracy, attempt or threat to commit any such act or *omission*, or being an accessory after the fact or counselling in relation to any such act or omission.[161] [My emphasis]

The Australian definition is also similar in its approach, where the Criminal Code 1995 was amended by the Security Legislation Amendment (Terrorism) Act 2002, meaning that the action must be taken to advance a political, religious or ideological cause aimed at influencing or intimidating a government Australian or foreign, or intimidating the public or a section of the

---

[160] See the Canadian Criminal Code R.S.C.1985, c. C-46, s83.01(1)(a) and (b)(i)(A) and (B), (ii)(A) to (E).
[161] *Ibid.*

public.[162] The Australian legislation, similar to the Canadian model, also omits action taken by way of protest, dissent or industrial action.[163] Rather than following these examples of higher bars, the UK has, in fact, gone further in lowering the bar by effectively removing the necessity for an action to influence the Government or international organization if section 1(3) of the Terrorism Act 2000 is satisfied. It contains an exclusionary provision for the use of firearms and explosives.[164] This augments the UK's definition of terrorism, changing to:

…the use or threat of action involving firearms or explosives, made for the purpose of advancing a political, religious, racial or ideological cause.

At first glance, the importance of this provision might be questioned, given the obviousness that such destructive methods and actions must be considered terrorism. It is argued, however, that this serves to over-complicate the definition of terrorism and augment it

---

[162] Criminal Code 1995, s 100.1(b) and (c)(i) and (c)(ii).
[163] Criminal Code 1995, s 100.3(a).
[164] Terrorism Act 2000, s 1(1)(b).

unnecessarily. It is irrelevant and unnecessary given that such action would most certainly serve to intimidate the public or section of the public in any regard.[165] Similar to the proliferation of causes, it adds further convolution to an already complex definition, unnecessarily stretching the applicability of the terrorist label.[166] As an example, should a citizen decide to threaten (i.e. the use or threat of action) a bank manager with a firearm (i.e. involving firearms or explosives) for the purposes of having the bank cancel all existing debt of all local citizens' (i.e. made for the purpose of advancing and ideological cause), the terrorist label here could potentially be ascribed. Thus, one could argue the provision removes the triadic nature of terrorism, thereby supporting Hacker's earlier assertion that the terrorist label could move to the dyadic sphere.[167]

Anderson would disagree, however, that this provision unnecessarily stretches the applicability of the label. He also believes that although the significance of

---

[165] R. English (2010) *Terrorism: How to Respond*, (Oxford University Press) p.4.

[166] *Supra* as per C. H. Simmons and J. R. Mitch (2001) at 246. See also *Ibid* at p.90.

[167] *Supra* as per F. J. Hacker (1980) 143-159.

this provision may be small, effectively removing the target provision would directly counter the intention of the Terrorism Act 2000.[168] Confusingly, Anderson did, however, go on to recommend the removal of this provision in his 2014 report. He noted that he was not swayed by the argument put forward by the then Home Secretary Charles Clarke:

… [section 1(3)]…is to cover, for instance, an assassination in which the terrorist's motive might be less to put the public in fear, or to influence the Government, than to 'take out' the individual…[169]

Anderson further explains that there is no reason as to why such action should be seen as terrorism and not simply murder. Critically, he appears to have potentially overlooked the fact that this provision fits within the rather historical rationale used by the international community in attempting to define an act of terrorism.

---

[168] *Supra* as per D. Anderson (2014) p.89.
[169] *Ibid.*

An International Threat Needs International Co-operation: The Extra-Jurisdictional Effect of UK Law

The similarity between the legal definitions of terrorism between nation-states within the Commonwealth and the EU illustrates the international nature of the 21st-century terrorism threat. It also goes some way in illustrating the fact that international security is just as important as national (internal) security.[170] Simplifying the issues here, it has become clear over time that 21st-century terrorists do not recognize borders. Instead, they utilized the freedom of movement across the EU, for example, of not only themselves but also illicit goods such as firearms and drugs. The Charlie Hebdo terrorist incident in 2015 illustrates this point. The military-grade firearms used in that attack were purchased by the defendants as deactivated, meaning they could not fire a live round. Once purchased, they were sent across the EU and into the Balkan States, reactivated, and then sent to France. Legitimate, open trade and free movement

---

[170] *Supra* as per The RT Hon Lord Lloyd of Berwick (1996) Chapter 2 paragraph 2.4.

of goods, has of course led to the criminal exploitation of this, meaning the free movement of illegal goods. This fact renders such extra-jurisdictional provisions essential within the guise of international co-operation.[171] This legal similarity is pertinent when the policing and security services are monitoring electronic communications data between members of the same group communicating in different parts of the world, for example, UK Islamic State fighters in Iraq communicating with UK Islamic State members encouraging or planning attacks in the UK.

To internationalize the law, similar to other nation-states, of course, an extra-jurisdictional approach is introduced by way of section 1(4) of the Terrorism Act 2000. This states that an act of terrorism applies to one committed or planned in any state in the world, not just the UK. The definition of 'government' came under judicial scrutiny in both cases, *R v F* and *R v Gul*, where the UK Court of Appeal held that the phrase was not restricted to representative or democratic governments. Therefore, the court pressed the point and confirmed the

---

[171] *Ibid.*

phrase government applied to all countries, additionally and controversially, to those governed by tyrants and dictators.[172] It may be the case that the apprehension of the UK being known internationally as a safe haven for terrorists and supporters made its way from Parliamentarians to the judiciary.[173] Focusing on the case of *R v Gul,* his appeal against conviction for terrorist offences was based on a number of factors. Overall *Gul's* rather clever legal argumentation turned on his assertion that section 1 of the Terrorism Act 2000 was too broad given its inheritance:

1. The Terrorism Act 2000 intended to give effect to the UK's international treaty obligations, and the concept of terrorism in international law does not extend to military attacks by a non-state armed group against state, or inter-governmental organization, armed

---

[172] *R v F* [2007] EWCA Crim 243, [9], [16], and *R v Gul* [2012] EWCA Crim 280, [23], [51], and *R v Gul* [2013] UKSC 64, [42], and the Terrorism Act 2000 s 1(4)(d), '…"the government" means the government of the United Kingdom, of a Part of the United Kingdom, or a country other than the United Kingdom'.

[173] *R v F* [2007] EWCA Crim 243, [16] and *R v Gul* [2012] EWCA Crim 280 [51].

forces in the context of a non-international armed conflict, and that this limitation should be implied into the definition in section 1;

2. Rather closely connected, the second argument was based on the fact that it would be wrong to read the Terrorism Acts of 2000 or 2006 as criminalizing in the UK an act abroad unless that act would be regarded as criminal by international law norms;

3. The third argument raised by the appellant was that some qualifications must be read into the very wide words of section 1 of the Terrorism Act 2000.[174]

Unlike comparative nation states, the UK does not omit action taken during an international armed conflict. The first argument, therefore, is by and large correct. The International Convention for the Suppression of Terrorist Bombings in 1997 and the International Convention for the Suppression of the Financing of Terrorism in 1999 expressly excludes attacks by insurgents on military forces during internationally recognized armed conflicts.[175]

---

[174] [2012] UKSC 64, [24].

[175] [2012] UKSC 64, [52], See also Terrorism Act 2000 ss 62-64 that formed the basis of *Gul's* argument, that the

Additionally, the 1977 Additional Protocol I to the 1949 Geneva Conventions (protection is afforded within Article 14 of the UN Charter) specifically relates to international armed conflict, which has the effect of somewhat indemnifying insurgents fighting against occupation in exercising self-determination during international armed conflicts.[176]

Although omitting such action seems to come naturally to the international players, what does not come easy is trying to define terrorism as a crime in its own right. Of course, there have been many previous international attempts at creating a definition of terrorism, but to no avail. The UN General Assembly in 2012 still could not agree on the differences between terrorism and a 'legitimate struggle of peoples fighting in the exercise of their right to self-determination'.[177] For McKeever, this is

---

Terrorism Act 2000 and by extension the Terrorism Act 2006 should conform to the international norm, given they were enacted under the UK's international obligations. The second part focused on the criminalisation of terrorist actions being more comprehensive and wider in the UK than required by international norms, [2013] UKSC 64, [43], and *R v Gul* [2012] EWCA Crim 280, [19](i)(ii).

[176] *R v Gul* [2012] EWCA Crim 280, [28].
[177] *R v Gul* [2013] UKSC 64, [45]-[47].

difficult to reconcile. He confirms that 'both the general abhorrence for violence which is indiscriminate and/or actively targets civilians, with the acknowledgement that some forms of political oppression may be so unjust as to legitimate violent action by the oppressed'.[178] To deal with the freedom fighter conundrum and to secure an effective move forward, the International Community has attempted to focus on the wrongful nature of terrorism rather than on the intent.[179] So, for the criminal lawyer, the *actus rea* rather than the *mens rea* to some extent. As a result, subsequent conventions have adopted an operational and practical definition of a specific type of terrorist act. This means without referring to underlying motivational aspects or causes, be it for political or ideological purposes.[180] The primary focus is concentrated on non-

---

[178] *Supra* as per D. McKeever (2010) 114.

[179] A. Gioia (2006) *The UN Conventions on the Prevention and Suppression of International Terrorism,* in G. Nesi, ed., *International Cooperation in Counter-terrorism: The United Nations And Regional Organizations in the Fight Against Terrorism,* (Ashgate) p.4.

[180] A. Byrnes (2002) Apocalyptic Visions and the Law: The Legacy of September 11, *a professorial address by Byrnes at the ANU Law School for the Faculty's 'Inaugural and Valedictory Lecture Series'.*

state actors adopting a criminal law enforcement model to address the problem, with an emphasis on increasing global co-operation.[181]

What is extremely clear from the decisions taken by the UK judiciary, including the Supreme Court, is a reluctance to interfere with the legislative provisions. Such intervention, of course, could effectively serve to introduce legal change, allowing for some sort of freedom fighter exclusion.[182] The judiciary has firmly decided that the nature of the broad definition was known to the UK Parliament prior to enactment, and they have had the opportunity to revisit it as a result of the various independent reviewers of anti-terrorism legislation conclusions and recommendations.[183] It is entirely feasible to presume, in fact, that the UK law draftsman and Parliament may have included freedom fighter type exclusion if, at that time, the EU Council's Framework Decision in 2002 contained a similar provision. Regardless, as accepted by the Supreme Court numerous

---

[181] *Ibid.*
[182] [2013] UKSC 64, [33]-[38].
[183] *Ibid*, [39].

times throughout the ages and public law specialists, the UK Parliament is supreme and able to legislate on any matters it chooses.

Some experts within this area sometimes overlook the fact of parliamentary sovereignty. We find this in Coco's analysis, authored prior to the UK Supreme Court's findings in R v Gul. In fact, Coco supports Gul's arguments and raises several important issues, one of which proposes that the UK Court of Appeal should have interpreted the UK domestic legislation in light of current international frameworks.[184] However, his analysis appears to fall on the pretence that the UK Parliament cannot gold-plate international law and that UK courts, although not requested to do so in this case, can question the validity of Acts of Parliament. Historical case law has illustrated that the UK Parliament is Sovereign and therefore perfectly capable of gold-plating and constructing law on any matter it so chooses.[185] It is important to note the

---

[184] A. Coco (2013) The Mark of Cain, *Journal of International Criminal Justice* 11(2), 425.

[185] *R v Gul* [2012] UKSC 64, [53]. See also K. Syrett (2011) *The Foundations of Public Law, Principles and Problems of Power in the British Constitution* (Palgrave Macmillan) p.100,

capability of the UK Parliament, in creating unfettered extra-territorial provisions.[186] This is of course nothing new and it has been seen in other types of statues, such as section 72 of the Sexual Offences Act 2003 and section 1 of the War Damages Act 1965.[187] In fact, the only time an Act of Parliament could be challenged by the courts was when the UK was a member of the European Union. Then, if the legal matter in question is related to an EU provision, EU law would win. The only other instance would be if the UK statute contravenes the European Convention on Human Rights as per the Human Rights Act 1998.[188] Albeit the court's finding here would not be binding, it is recommendatory only.

Although a rather unpalatable suggestion, there is no defence in the UK, freedom fighter style or otherwise available for an accused to use within the terms under the

---

'Gold-plating' is the exercise that refers to the UK government legislating further than is required by international law.

[186] *R v Gul* [2012] EWCA Crim 280, [56], and *R v Gul* [2013] UKSC 64.

[187] *Madzimbamuto v Lardber-Burke* [1969] 1 AC 645, [723], See also *Supra* as per K. Syrett (2011) p.104.

[188] See *Mccartys Ltd. v Smith* [1980] ECR 1275 (Case 129/79) for EU law, and see *Gillan v UK* [2010] 50 EHRR 45 (4158/05) (echr) for European Convention on Human Rights.

Terrorism Act 2000, unlike other comparative jurisdictions. Put simply, the UK Parliamentarians and the judiciary appear to keep an arm's length from exempting what could be termed 'terrorism in a just cause'.[189] What is most interesting is that even if the state has such an exemption clause, the judiciary appears to be somewhat reluctant to use it. For example, we can look to the case of R v Khawaja, moving across Canada for the moment, where such an exemption exists. The Canadian judiciary here tested the armed conflict exclusion, where *Khawaja* claimed that the situation in Afghanistan since 2002 represented a war within the legal definition. This would, therefore, render his actions as being carried out during an armed conflict and in accordance with international law.[190] However, because Khawaja's actions involved acts of violence in the UK and Pakistan and were based on a violent Islamist ideology, the Court found his actions went beyond the Afghanistan conflict. The Court also held the conflict in Afghanistan did not represent a war. Instead,

---

[189] *Ibid*, [27]. See also *Supra* as per D. McKeever (2010) 113.

[190] [2012] SCC69, [2012] 3 S.C.R. 555.

they asserted that it represented an armed insurrection carried out based on violent jihad against the newly appointed Afghan government and non-Islamic regimes and civilians.[191] This illustrates that even when a state has a freedom fighter style defence, the tests applied by the judicial authority appear to be stringent and protective of maintaining the status quo. This analogy appears to fit with Netanyahu's postulation that freedom fighters are, in fact, not capable of perpetrating terrorist acts:

In contrast to the terrorists, no freedom fighter has ever deliberately attacked innocents. He has never deliberately killed small children, passers-by in the street, foreign visitors, or other civilians who happen to reside in the area of conflict or are merely associated ethnically or religiously with the people of that area...The conclusion we must draw from all this is evident. Far from being a bearer of freedom, the terrorist is the carrier of oppression and enslavement.[192]

---

[191] *Ibid*, [100], [102].

[192] B. Netanyahu (1985) *Terrorism: How the West Can Win*. (Farrar, Strauss and Giroux, New York) p.27.

The facts discussed in the case of *Gul*, however, highlight that even if a freedom fighter exclusion did exist within the UK's legislative framework, it would have made little difference to the outcome. It also suggests the unimportance of the UK Court seeking advice as to whether or not the conflicts were to be regarded as an international armed conflict, given *Gul* posted a video containing not only attacks on Coalition forces but also civilians that were in the US twin towers on 11th September 2001 at the time of al-Qaeda's attack. It also included other attacks on civilians and excerpts from martyrdom videos with symbols associated with proscribed organizations listed under Schedule 2 of the 2000 Act.[193] Despite these facts, the Court thought there was a need to elucidate further, confirming international law had developed insofar as criminalizing terrorism in times of peace.[194] International Humanitarian Law and International Criminal Law specifically refer to civilians and organized groups within their definition and cover

---

[193] *R v Gul* [2012] EWCA Crim 280, [6], [20](1)(2). See also Terrorism Act 2000, s 3(1)(a) and Schedule 2.
[194] *Ibid*, [33].

acts of terrorism during an international armed conflict.[195] Defining terrorism as an act carried out primarily against civilians, international rules such as those provided by Article 33(1) of the Fourth Geneva Convention effectively ban terrorism, with other conventions considering it to be a war crime.[196]

What is clear from the UK court's decision in not allowing a freedom fighter defence is finding it unpalatable the idea of branding some types of terrorism as officially acceptable:

...acts by insurgents against the armed forces of a state anywhere in the world which seek to influence a government...made for political purposes is terrorism. There is no exemption for those engaged in an armed insurrection and an armed struggle against a government.[197]

---

[195] A. Cassese (2008) *International Criminal Law* (2nd Edition, Oxford University Press) p.171.

[196] Fourth Geneva Convention 1949: 'terrorist acts are prohibited if perpetrated by civilians or organised groups in occupied territories or in the territory of a party to the conflict'. See also: Second Additional Protocol 1977, article 4(1), 4(2)(d), 13(2), 51(2). See also *Ibid* pp.171-173.

[197] *R v Gul* [2012] EWCA Crim 280, [16].

While this statement may bolster Coco's argument, it appears to imply that the courts possess universal jurisdiction over terrorism.[198] In response to such criticism, the UK Court of Appeal referenced the Lotus case, adjudicated by the Permanent Court of International Justice. This case affirmed that the court's jurisdiction was not in question due to the absence of explicit prohibitions against labelling non-state armed groups' attacks on state armed forces as terrorism in non-international armed conflicts.[199] Additionally, although the former UK Foreign Secretary's testimony confirmed the conflicts in Afghanistan and Iraq during 2008 and 2009 as non-international armed conflicts, thereby undermining *Gul's* argument, the judicial decision's impact reinforces the UK Government's commitment to the international effort to combat terrorism and serves to deter individuals from planning actions to occur on foreign soil from the UK.[200]

---

[198] *Supra* as per A. Coco (2013).

[199] *S. S. Lotus (France v Turkey)* [1927] PCIJ Series A, No 10, [44], and *R v Gul* [2012] EWCA Crim 280, [47]-[49].

[200] *R v F* [2007] EWCA Crim 243, [9], [16], and *R v Gul* [2012] EWCA Crim 280, [20], [23], [28], [51], and *R v Gul* [2013] UKSC 64. See also A. Murray (2012) Acts of was or acts

This mirrors the approach taken by the UK Government during the drafting of the Terrorism Act 2000. The aim of protecting foreign governments from terrorism planned and organized in the UK was further reinforced by the Crime (International Co-operation) Act 2003, which states that a resident in the UK would be guilty of an offense if actions abroad would constitute an offense within the UK under the Terrorism Act 2000.[201]

It is, in fact, quite instructive to see where the UK Government stands should a citizen return from fighting in Syria or Iraq with Kurdish forces against the Islamic State, given this has not been recognized as an international armed conflict.[202] During the height of the Islamic State's power, numerous UK citizens departed the country to join Kurdish forces engaged in combat against

---

of terrorism? Case Comment, *Journal of Criminal Law,* 76(4), 298-302, 299.

[201] Crime (International Co-operation) Act 2003, s 63A-E. Terrorism Act 2000 ss 54, 56-61.

[202] E. Saner (2015) Brits abroad: is it against the law to fight ISIS? The Guardian, 25 February 2015, available at https://www.theguardian.com/world/shortcuts/2015/feb/25/brits-abroad-against-law-fight-isis accessed 15 February 2024.

the Islamic State's stronghold in areas like Mosul.[203] However, the classification of these individuals as terrorists varies depending on the country and the group they join.[204] For instance, Turkey considers British citizens fighting with the YPG (People's Protection Units) as terrorists, particularly due to Turkey's conflict with the Kurdish group PKK, which seeks independence for Kurdish territory from Turkey. Under Section 3 and Schedule 2 of the Terrorism Act 2000, the PKK is a proscribed group in the UK, thus considered a terrorist organization. However, the YPG and YPJ in Syria, which are the armed factions of the Syrian Kurds and were fighting against the Islamic State and the al-Assad regime,

---

[203] See http://www.bbc.co.uk/news/world-middle-east-33083213 and http://www.bbc.co.uk/news/world-middle-east-33083256 accessed 15 February 2024.

[204] S. Sharma and A. MacDonald (2016) British volunteers in Syrian Kurd forces are 'terrorists', Turkey says. Middle East Eye, 1 September 2016, available at http://www.middleeasteye.net/news/turkey-british-ypg-terrorist-syria-874419624 accessed 15 February 2024. See also I. Drury (2015) Public schoolboy who quit City to fight ISIS returns home: Briton who spent five months alongside Kurdish forces says he can justify actions if questioned by police, Mail Online, 10 June 2015, available at http://www.dailymail.co.uk/news/article-3119071/ISIS-fighting-city-trader-returns-home-UK.html accessed 15 February 2024.

are not proscribed in the UK. Consequently, any UK citizen joining the YPG/YPJ would not be labelled a terrorist, and the actions of this group are not considered terrorist activities in the UK.[205] Turkey, on the other hand, sees the YPG/YPJ as simply PKK factions and classes them also as terrorists. However, the YPG/YPJ is not a proscribed group in the UK; therefore, fighting with them is not deemed to be a terrorist action, despite Turkey's position on this subject.

During the debates on the Terrorism Act 2000, concerns were raised about the absence of a provision that would allow for a defence akin to that of a freedom

---

[205] For current list of UK proscribed organisations: https://www.gov.uk/government/uploads/system/uploads/attachm ent_data/file/578385/201612_Proscription.pdf. See also C. Davies (2015) Girl becomes first Briton convicted of trying to join fight against Islamic State in Syria, The Guardian, 20 November 2015, available at https://www.theguardian.com/uk-news/2015/nov/20/girl-becomes-first-briton-convicted-of-trying-to-join-fight-against-islamic-state-in-syria and http://thekurdishproject.org/history-and-culture/kurdish-nationalism/pkk-kurdistan-workers-party/ accessed 15 February 2024. See also M. Blake (2017) Blackburn activisty becomes first British woman to join fight against ISIS in Syria, The Guardian, available at https://www.theguardian.com/uk-news/2017/feb/09/blackburn-activist-kimberly-taylor-becomes-first-british-woman-join-fight-isis-syria accessed 15 February 2024.

fighter. Parliamentarians specifically discussed the potential ambiguity of the terms used in the Act and whether the lack of such a provision would unfairly criminalize individuals who could be considered modern equivalents of the Suffragettes or the South African opponents of apartheid.[206] Sir Igor Judge in *R v F* appeared to have proffered caution in not permitting some defence typology:

The call for resistance to tyranny and invasion evokes an echoing response down the ages. We note, as a matter of historical knowledge, that many of those whose violent activities in support of national independence or freedom from oppression, who were once described as terrorists, are now honoured as 'freedom fighters'.[207]

---

[206] A. W. Bradley and K. D. Ewing (2011) *Constitutional and Administrative Law*, (15th Edition, Pearson Education Ltd) p.590. See also C. Walker (2008) Terrorism: Terrorism Act 2000 ss. 1 and 58 – possession of terrorist documents, Case Comment, *Criminal Law Review* [2008] 160-165, 162. Suffragettes were members of women's organisations in the late 19th and early 20th century that advocated the extension of the "franchise", or the right to vote in public elections, to women.

[207] *R v F* [2007] EWCA Crim 243, [9].

Although acknowledging this, the Court held, '...terrorism is terrorism, whatever the motives of the perpetrators'.[208] The Government unsurprisingly rejected Igor Judge's statement. This prompted Lord Carlile, who was the independent reviewer of anti-terrorism legislation in 2007, to propose a statutory obligation that would compel the executive to examine the nature and target of the action, as well as international legal obligations, before initiating criminal charges.[209] Walker proffers a rather scathing view for not creating or allowing a type of freedom fighter defence or exception where he states:

...an antidote to the trend that the UK Government values friendship with oil-owning despots much more highly than the political freedom exercised by refugee underdogs.[210]

Even though international conventions exist, the UK Court of Appeal highlighted the absence of a universally accepted definition of terrorism. Despite being revisited

---

[208] *Ibid*, [9] and [27].
[209] *Supra* as per Lord Carlile of Berriew Q.C. (2007) paragraph 58.
[210] *Supra* as per C. Walker (2008) 165.

by the Member States of the UN in 2002 and 2004, the deadlock in the negotiations centred on whether such a definition would apply to a state's armed forces (state terrorism) and to liberation movements (freedom fighters).[211] Regarding the latter issue, this poses a challenge domestically, as highlighted by the UK judiciary, because if violent actions or threats by individuals involved in armed conflicts abroad were to be differentiated, they would no longer be considered terrorism.[212] The UK judiciary has shown that although International Humanitarian Law prohibits deliberate targeting of civilians and could constitute a war crime, such prosecutions are highly unusual.[213] The UK Court of Appeals decision follows such concern, where it was held that the conflicts in Afghanistan and Iraq were both regarded as non-international armed conflicts, thereby

---

[211] T, Deen, (2005) U.N. Member States Struggle to Define Terrorism, Inter Press Service, see http://www.ipsnews.net/2005/07/politics-un-member-states-struggle-to-define-terrorism/ accessed 15 February 2024.

[212] *R v Gul* [2012] EWCA Crim 280, [23], and *R v Gul* [2013] UKSC 64, [42].

[213] *Supra* as per D. Anderson (2014) p.26.

removing the possibility of a claim for combatant immunity for legitimate insurgency.

The UK Discretionary Power to Prosecute

Possibly offering some relief from the overly broad definition of terrorism, the executive functions can provide some moderation before formal charges are brought. According to section 117 of the Terrorism Act 2000, the consent of the Director of Public Prosecutions (DPP) is required before proceedings can be initiated.[214] However, the discretionary power granted to the DPP was criticized by the UK Supreme Court in R v Gul as "intrinsically unattractive," as it amounted to the legislature relinquishing prosecutorial powers to an unelected, albeit respected and independent lawyer.[215] The Court emphasized the risk of undermining the rule of law, noting that while the DPP is accountable to Parliament, decisions made in an open and democratically accountable manner are not made in the same manner and form as

---

[214] Terrorism Act 2000, s 117(2)(a).
[215] *R v Gul* [2013] UKSC 64, [35]-[36].

those in Parliament.[216] It is important to note that other aspects of UK criminal law also have broad definitions that the DPP oversees. In practice, this system seems to function quite effectively.[217]

The Sexual Offences Act 2003 serves as an example of this, as section 4 removed the ability for persons under 16 to consent to sexual activity.[218] Consequently, two individuals under the age of 16 would both be guilty of an offense, as they are legally unable to consent.[219] In a similar vein, the then Home Secretary reassured Parliamentarians that the term 'ideological' in the 2000 Act would not encompass industrial action, indicating that charges would not be brought against children under 16 engaging in consensual sexual activity.[220] While this statement is somewhat ambiguous, such criticism is beyond the scope of the current discussion. The Crown Prosecution Service

---

[216] *Ibid.*

[217] Such as the Sexual Offences Act 2003.

[218] See http://www.cps.gov.uk/legal/p_to_r/rape_and_sexual_offences/consent/ accessed 15 February 2024.

[219] D. Ormerod (2008) *Smith and Hogan Criminal Law* (12th Edition, Oxford University Press) pp.706-708.

[220] *Ibid.*

has since issued guidance to emphasize that 'it was not Parliament's intention to punish children unnecessarily'.[221] This type of safeguarding power could also be used to narrow the definition of 'Government' within the terrorism definition, potentially allowing for a freedom fighter exclusion, at least to some extent.. Given the extremely broad nature of the Terrorism Act 2000, it is argued that without this safeguard, the law could potentially be used inappropriately. It is further contended that although the DPP safeguard is useful, it does not replace legislative certainty.

What is the Political Value of Terrorism, and does it outweigh the rule of law?

The consequences of this legislative ambiguity become apparent when political influence and the political significance of terrorism overshadow its legal definition, making its application challenging in legal discussions.[222]

---

[221]*Supra* as per http://www.cps.gov.uk/legal/p_to_r/rape_and_sexual_offences/consent/ accessed 15 February 2024.

[222] S. Zeidan (2004) Desperately Seeking Definition: The International Community's Quest for Identifying the Specter of Terrorism, *Cornell International Law Journal*, Volume 36, Issue

On an international scale, and perhaps domestically as well, when left to its political interpretation, terrorism can undergo significant changes to align with the interests of a specific state and government at a given time.[223] For this reason, it is argued that the law should take precedence and establish a clear and precise legal stance, stripping terrorism of its political currency that is often based on historical associations.[224] Gale argues that the lack of precision in defining terrorism undermines the principle of due process of law, which holds that the law should be as precise and foreseeable as possible, as established in the cases of *Steel and others v United Kingdom*, and, *Hashman and*

3, Article 5, 491-496, 491-492. See also: *Supra* as per B. Saul (2006) at p.3.

[223] *Ibid.*

[224] The political value can be seen historically during the Peninsula Wars of 1809-1813, evidenced more recently where the Taliban and Osama bin Laden represented the US in Afghanistan, seen as President Regan's freedom fighters (Mujahideen) and supported by the US Central Intelligence Agency (CIA), where they were resisting the Soviet occupation. They changed however, to President Bush Jnr's terrorists particularly after 2001. See G. Chaliand (1987) *Terrorism: From Popular Struggle to Media Spectacle* (London: Saqi Books) p.37. See also *Supra* as per C. Walker (2009) at p.1. See also *Supra* as per S. Zeidan (2004) 492.

Harrup v United Kingdom.[225] This issue is particularly pronounced in the international context, where the challenge of establishing an objective legal definition is compounded by the existence of two distinct terms for terrorism: one used by states and another for freedom fighters.[226] While the topics of state terrorism and counter-insurgency are not within the scope of this book, it is worth noting Marian Price, a convicted IRA terrorist, has commented on this particular issue:

I don't see any distinction between al-Qaeda and what George [W] Bush's pilots did in Afghanistan. I would equate those two as terror because that's what they are designed to do…to terrorize a population into surrender. That's the real terrorism.[227]

The divergence in viewpoints highlights the inherent subjectivity of the label and demonstrates that the politically charged term can extend beyond its legal

---

[225] *Supra* as per C. J. S. Gale, (2006). *Steel and others v United Kingdom* [1999] 28 EHRR 603 [54] and; *Hashman and Harrup v United Kingdom* [2000] EHRR 241 [31].

[226] *Supra* as per S. Zeidan (2004) 494-495.

[227] *Supra* as per R. English (2010) at p.20.

definition.[228] This also underscores the potential for extensive misuse of the term, leading to confusion surrounding the concept.[229]

Conclusion

The UK's legal definition of terrorism under the Terrorism Act 2000 faces two primary issues. Firstly, there is a definitional problem as the phrases used by Parliament remain relatively undefined. This has led to challenges in determining which phrase applies to a specific case, thus affecting judicial application to some extent. The second issue, related to the first, concerns the political

---

[228] *Supra* as per C. Walker (2009) at p.3, See also *Supra* as per B. Saul (2006) at p.3.

[229] *Ibid* as per B. Saul (2006) at p.3. See also W. Laqueur (1987) *The Age of Terrorism* (Boston: Little, Brown and Company) p.143. See also: M. Freeman (2005) *Order, Rights and Threats: Terrorism and Global Justice*, in R. A. Wilson (ed) *Human Rights in the War on Terror* (Cambridge University Press). For example see United Nations ComHR preambles in 1998/47, 1999/27, 2000/30, 2001/31, 2002/35. It has also been made clear that terrorist activity cannot be used as a means to protect human rights. See A. Byrnes (2002) Apocalyptic Visions and the Law: The Legacy of September 11, a professorial address by Byrnes at the ANU Law School for the Faculty's *Inaugural and Valedictory Lecture Series*, May 30, 2002, available at https://law.anu.edu.au/CIPL/StaffPapersTalks&Submissions/Byrn es30May02.pdf accessed 15 February 2024.

connotations of the term's use. To address this, the UK could redefine terrorism to eliminate various political references. This could be accompanied by the introduction of exclusion clauses for actions taken as protest, industrial action, or dissent or during an international armed conflict in line with customary international law. While the UK's legal definition of terrorism has shown reasonable effectiveness in practice, the lack of definitional certainty increases its political significance and invites criticisms based on the rule of law. To address this, the UK should align the definition of terrorism with international law and comparative practices. For instance, it could be defined as follows: 'Terrorism' is the use or threat of serious violence intended to compel a government or an international organization unduly or to seriously intimidate the public or a section thereof for the purpose of advancing a political, religious, ideological, or racial cause. Protest, dissent, or industrial action is not included in this definition. Action taken during an armed conflict as part of a legitimate struggle of peoples fighting in the exercise of their right to self-determination is not terrorism, unless such action is directed towards non-combatants and/or civilians.

Chapter Two: Why Pre-Emptive Counter-terrorism Measures are Needed

Introduction

The increasing independent operational abilities of terrorists gained through online information or training in conflict areas add to the arguably unquantifiable threat they pose.

This chapter will further emphasize the necessity of mass data collection and pre-emptive legislative measures to mitigate the terrorist threat. It will focus on measures such as temporary travel restrictions and the criminalization of neutral behaviours, like collecting data deemed useful to terrorists. While discussing the interconnectedness of risk society theory and predictive policing, the chapter will remain within the legal research framework, debunking terms like 'mass data surveillance' and 'pre-crime.' It will clarify that data retention is distinct from mass surveillance and that 'pre-crime' is a misleading term, as pre-emptive measures are actually criminal offenses.

The chapter will demonstrate the need for pre-emptive measures, as current counter-terrorism legislation has not effectively countered terrorist propaganda or infiltrated encrypted electronic communications data.

The sudden increase in independent operational abilities may stem from the abundance of extremist material available on the internet. Alternatively, individuals may have travelled to other countries for terrorist training, a phenomenon referred to as 'Jihadi tourism' by UK law enforcement services.[230] Reports indicate that approximately 5000 EU citizens have been or are currently involved in terrorist-related activities in conflict zones like Somalia, Syria, Iraq, Libya, and Yemen. It is estimated that one in 15 returning individuals suspected of terrorist involvement may pose a threat to their respective national states upon their return.[231] However, the methodology used to calculate these figures

---

[230] Supra as per The Rt. Hon. Sir Malcolm Rifkind MP (2014) p.6.

[231] G. Buttarelli (2015) Counter-terrorism, De-Radicalisation and Foreign Fighters', Joint debate during the extraordinary meeting of the LIBE Committee. European Parliament, Brussels, 27 January 2015.

is unknown, primarily due to the challenge of gathering accurate data, compounded by the fact that the information comes from UK security services and is classified. Consequently, it is argued that these estimates could be significantly higher or lower, rendering the terror threat unquantifiable.

The finite nature of resources compounds the already challenging task of monitoring potential terrorists and suspects, making it exceedingly difficult, if not impossible, to manage the risk accurately.

Islamist or Jihadi tourism presents its own dangers, not only enhancing independent operational abilities but also providing extensive hands-on military training in firearms and explosives.[232] Although traveling to conflict zones increases the likelihood of individuals being known to law enforcement agencies, the risk remains somewhat unquantifiable. Rifkind's 2014 report indicates that the independent operational abilities, combined with the methods used by lone actors and self-starting terrorists, offer fewer opportunities for security services to detect

---

[232] *Ibid.*

their activity.[233] As the nature of threats evolves, the practices and policies necessary for prevention must also change to reflect these threats.[234] Recognizing the mounting, diversifying, and increasingly complex threats, there has been a sudden growth in risk management styles employed by police and security services when assessing intelligence.[235]

Due to the effective marketing and promotion of IS, a significant number of foreign fighters have travelled to Syria and Iraq. According to the National Counter-terrorism Centre Director, as of October 2015, IS had 'attracted more than 28,000 foreign fighters, including at least 5,000 westerners'.[236]

---

[233] *Supra* as per The Rt. Hon. Sir Malcolm Rifkind MP (2014) p.82.

[234] J. G. Carter and D. L. Carter (2012) Law enforcement intelligence: implications for self-radicalized terrorism, Police Practice and Research, 13:2, 138-154, 138.

[235] *Supra* as per The Rt. Hon. Sir Malcolm Rifkind MP (2014) pp.81-82.

[236] See http://www.bbc.co.uk/news/world-middle-east-29052144 accessed 15 February 2024.

Dr Simon Hale-Ross

What is Jihadi Tourism? Passport and Travel Document Seizure

Counter-Terrorism and Security Act 2015

To address and prevent UK citizens from leaving the country to engage in terrorist-related activities, the Counter-Terrorism and Security Act 2015 (CTSA) introduced additional pre-emptive measures. The CTSA also aimed to prevent the return of citizens who had trained and fought with terrorist groups abroad. The primary pre-emptive power is outlined in Part 1, Chapter 1 of the CTSA, which allows law enforcement agencies to seize passports and travel documents from individuals suspected of involvement in terrorism. Schedule One of the CTSA specifies that passports can be retained for up to 14 days from the day after the initial seizure. Although initially a short-term measure, this time frame can be extended with judicial approval to 30 days from the day after the initial seizure. Judicial approval is required, and the Secretary of State must demonstrate that relevant individuals have acted diligently and expeditiously concerning the matters.

These provision were debated heavily during the enactment stages that led Lord Carlile to state:

We heard some criticism of Clause 1, but I say... [Lordships] have got to get real about what Clause 1 is dealing with. Let me give you [a hypothetical] example...Suppose a suspicious travel agent who is public spirited telephones the police and says, 'I have just sold an air ticket in suspicious circumstances', and the authorities decide it is worth following the person who has bought the air ticket. That kind of incident can occur within an hour, and it does not leave the time to go to a judge to get permission to seize that passport. We have to allow the authorities to deal with the urgent provisions made in Clause 1 and Schedule 1.[237]

Following this example and given that according to Rowley, the Metropolitan Police Assistant Commissioner, at the very least, a total of 700 UK citizens have traveled to Syria, with apparently more than half having returned to the UK, where they now pose a significant threat. Therefore, the urgency and requirement for such emergency power can be appreciated.[238] While the time limitations are not too restrictive, there is still the issue of due process and the impact upon the individual's privacy, particularly their Article 45 right of the EU Charter, Freedom of movement and residence.[239]

---

[237] Lord Carlile of Berriew, Counter-Terrorism and Security Bill 2015, House of Lords Second Reading Stage, (13 January 2024: Column 722 7.27pm).

[238] P. Wintour (2015) *UK parents to get power to cancel children's passports over Isis fears*, The Guardian, 20 July 2015, available at https://www.theguardian.com/politics/2015/jul/20/uk-parents-power-cancel-childrens-passports-isis-fears accessed 24 January 2024.

[239] Charter of Fundamental Rights of the European Union, see: http://eur-lex.europa.eu/legal-content/EN/TXT/?uri=CELEX:12012P/TXT accessed 1 January 2024. 'The free movement of persons is a fundamental right guaranteed by the EU to its citizens'. It entitles every EU citizen to travel, work and live in any EU country without special

As with European Convention on Human Rights, any restriction on exercising rights and freedoms under the Charter must be established by law.[240] The principle of proportionality is the ultimate criterion, and it must be considered necessary to achieve recognized Union

---

formalities. [Although the UK is not a member of Schengen]…Schengen cooperation enhances this freedom by enabling citizens' to cross-internal borders without being subjected to border checks. The border-free Schengen Area guarantees free movement to more than 400 million EU citizens', as well as to many non-EU nationals, businessmen, tourists or other persons legally present on the EU territory.' See http://ec.europa.eu/dgs/home-affairs/what-we-do/policies/borders-and-visas/schengen/index_en.htm accessed 1 January 2024. And see also: 'Free movement of workers is a fundamental principle of the Treaty enshrined in Article 45 of the Treaty on the Functioning of the European Union and developed by EU secondary legislation and the Case law of the Court of Justice.' http://ec.europa.eu/social/main.jsp?catId=457 accessed 15 February 2024..

[240] Charter of Fundamental Rights of the European Union, Article 52(1).

objectives or to safeguard the rights and freedoms of others. These measures not only safeguard the public at large but also protect vulnerable young adults and children from being exposed to and influenced by terrorist-related activities if they were allowed to leave.

The provisions under Schedule One are wide in nature and define involvement in terrorism-related activity as:

(a) the commission, preparation, or instigation of acts of terrorism;

(b) conduct that facilitates the commission, preparation, or instigation of such acts or is intended to do so;

(c) conduct that gives encouragement to the commission, preparation, or instigation of such acts or is intended to do so;

(d) conduct that gives support or assistance to individuals who are known or believed by the person concerned to be involved in conduct falling within paragraph; (a) It is immaterial whether the acts of terrorism in question are specific acts of terrorism or acts of terrorism in general.'[241]

Suppose a constable or qualified officer has reasonable grounds to suspect that a person is departing the UK for the purpose of engaging in terrorism-related activities or has arrived and is about to leave the UK for such purposes. In that case, several powers are provided under Schedule 1, paragraph 2(5):

(a) to require the person to hand over all travel documents in his or her possession to the constable or (as the case may be) the qualified officer;

(b) to search for travel documents relating to the person and to take possession of any that the constable or officer finds;

(c) to inspect any travel document relating to the person;

(d) to retain any travel document relating to the person that is lawfully in the possession of the constable or officer.

---

[241] Counter-Terrorism and Security Act 2015, Schedule 1, paragraph 1(10).

To retain the travel documents for the specified length of time, a senior officer's authorization must be attained.[242] The documents can then be retained while the Secretary of State considers the case.[243] They can also be retained while the authorities consider charging the citizen with an offense or subjecting them to further measures.[244] A person who fails to hand over all travel documentation or obstruct the process may be liable to six months imprisonment if found guilty of the offense.[245] The issue here is that the citizen may request a judicial review of the decision to retain his passport; however, the intelligence and evidence gathered may be withheld from the suspect.[246] This makes it almost impossible for a citizen to, in fact, make a reviewable argument.

---

[242] Counter-Terrorism and Security Act 2015, Schedule 1, paragraph 4(1)(a).

[243] Counter-Terrorism and Security Act 2015, Schedule 1, paragraph 5(1)(a).

[244] Counter-Terrorism and Security Act 2015, Schedule 1, paragraph 5(1)(b)(c).

[245] Counter-Terrorism and Security Act 2015, Schedule 1, paragraph 15(1)(2)(3).

[246] Counter-Terrorism and Security Act 2015, Schedule 1, paragraph 10(2), dealing with the extension period to 30 days.

Temporary Exclusion Orders

The UK, by way of Part 1 Chapter 2 of the CTSA, fashions further intrusive pre-emptive measures aimed at preventing highly trained and militarily hardened terrorists from returning to the UK, who may then pose a direct or indirect risk to national security. Termed 'temporary exclusion orders' they state:

(1) A temporary exclusion order is an order which requires an individual not to return to the United Kingdom unless-

   (a) the return is in accordance with a permit to return issued by the Secretary of State before the individual began the return or

   (b) the return is the result of the individual's deportation to the UK.

Five conditions must be met before an order by the Secretary of State can be made and the order lasts up to two years.[247]

---

[247] Counter-Terrorism and Security Act 2015, s 4(3)(b) limits the temporary exclusion orders to 2 years inclusive.

It is crucial to note that the Secretary of State must have reasonable grounds to suspect that the individual is or has been involved in terrorism-related activity outside the UK and must reasonably consider it necessary, for purposes related to protecting UK citizens from terrorism, to impose a temporary exclusion order on the individual.[248] The UK Court can grant the Secretary of State permission to make an order under section 3, or the Secretary of State can argue that the case's urgency requires a temporary exclusion order to be imposed without obtaining permission.[249] The Act grants extensive powers to the executive, but there are some safeguards for the citizen through judicial supervision.

Firstly, the Secretary of State must provide a statement outlining the urgency of the case and the necessity for the order to be imposed without obtaining the court's permission. Notice of the order must be given to the court immediately after the temporary exclusion order is imposed, and the court must review the decision within 7

---

[248] Counter-Terrorism and Security Act 2015, Chapter 2.
[249] Counter-Terrorism and Security Act 2015, Chapter 2(7)(b).

days of the order being made. If the court is satisfied with the urgency of the order, they must affirm the imposition; however, if the court finds the order flawed, they can quash it.[250]

Judicial supervision, somewhat similar to that found in the Investigatory Powers Act 2016, is to be welcomed as a safeguarding development. Some other safeguarding clauses, such as the two-year limitation, were debated heavily during the enactment stages, leading Lord Carlile to state:

I do not understand the two years contained in these amendments. The issue we are dealing with and covered in this clause is, unfortunately, going to last for more than two years...having a two-year sunset clause...would send out a completely incorrect message to those who are minded to go abroad and participate in jihad...We have to show some enduring determination over this issue.[251]

---

[250] Counter-Terrorism and Security Act 2015, Schedule 2, paragraph 4.

[251] Lord Carlile of Berriew, Counter-Terrorism and Security Bill 2015, House of Lords First Committee Stage, (20 January 2015: Column 1212).

Although the European Convention on Human Rights and the EU Charter rights under Union law appear to have lacked discussion, the Marquess of Lothian raised a valid concern:

...looking at the time factor here, what is the legal and international status of someone who has been subjected to a temporary exclusion order?[252]

This question is relevant due to the legal and practical implications for the citizens subjected to this type of order. It is important to note that the order is temporary, not indefinite, and therefore does not render the person stateless. The UK is a signatory to two United Nations Conventions that prevent a State from rendering a citizen stateless: the Convention Relating to the Status of Stateless Persons 1954 and the 1961 Convention on the Reduction of Statelessness. The 1961 Convention is an international instrument that protects citizens from inappropriate and unfair threats of statelessness.[253]

---

[252] Marquess of Lothian, Counter-Terrorism and Security Bill 2015, House of Lords First Committee Stage, (20 January 2015: Column 1213).
[253] See http://www.unhcr.org/pages/4a2535c3d.html accessed 15 February 2024.

What is intriguing, however, is that the Home Secretary, using Royal Prerogative power, can already revoke UK citizenship entitlement, provided the individual holds dual nationality.[254] In light of the current terrorist threat, the necessity for this type of power to be codified in law is evident. This is where the then Prime Minister David Cameron's choice of words could be examined; he described the actions of UK citizens fighting for the Islamic State as disloyal. Articles 8 and 9 of the 1961 Convention explicitly prohibit the deprivation of nationality based on racial, ethnic, religious, or political grounds. Although the religious beliefs and political aspirations exhibited by members of Islamic State are abhorrent, they would appear to fall within this definition.[255]

---

[254] See http://www.findlaw.co.uk/law/government/constitutional_law/citizens_guide_to_government/500456.html accessed 15 February 2024.
[255] See http://www.independent.co.uk/news/world/middle-east/who-are-isis-the-rise-of-the-islamic-state-in-iraq-and-the-levant-9541421.html accessed 15 February 2024.

However, under the Convention, if a citizen has committed acts inconsistent with the duty of loyalty to the State, the State retains the right to deprive that citizen of nationality, even if this results in statelessness. One could argue that the actions of the Islamic State terrorists are certainly inconsistent with the UK. Additionally, Article 19 of the EU Charter prohibits collective expulsion or the expulsion of a person to a State where there is a risk of torture, the death penalty, or other inhuman or degrading treatment. Although constrained by law, it is argued that this particular aspect of the UK's legislative measure will increasingly come under judicial scrutiny.

For example, the Court of Justice of the European Union is not disinclined in striking down disproportionate measures, particularly when such citizens' could be permitted to return to the UK and subjected to other forms of pre-terrorism sanctions in accordance with other existing legislative measures.[256] Lord Macdonald of River Glaven appears to have at least recognized the impact of

---

[256] Terrorism Prevention and Investigation Measures Act 2011, s 2, and the extension to these measures brought about by the Counter-Terrorism and Security Act 2015, s 16.

these measures and the potential for such friction between the executive and the courts:

...we should not give away our freedoms in response to terrorism...[it] would be a good idea if [we] were to include a sunset clause...[because the] practicalities of this measure—how it will work in practice—...are most in doubt. Those practicalities will significantly impact the rights of people on whom the orders are imposed...I support the idea of a sunset clause so that the House can thoroughly review how the legislation works in practice.[257]

The mere suspicion that a citizen has engaged in terrorism-related activity is the required threshold. Given the duration and intrusiveness of temporary exclusion orders, the threshold for imposing them should be higher, requiring the executive to be convinced that the citizen would pose a serious threat upon their return. The decision is subject to review and can be appealed by the citizen, but the same rules regarding disclosure apply to

---

[257] Lord Macdonald of River Glaven, Counter-Terrorism and Security Bill 2015, House of Lords First Committee Stage, (20 January 2015: Column 1214).

the removal of passports and travel documents.[258] The potential consequences for a citizen returning to the UK after a temporary exclusion order has been issued are severe; if found guilty of an offense, they could be sentenced to up to 5 years in prison.[259]

The UK Government is clearly making efforts to mitigate the terrorist risk, as it is their responsibility to protect life and ensure the safety of their citizens. These powers are still relatively new, so there is limited data on how they function in practice. In 2015, Germany adopted a similar approach to the UK in attempting to prevent jihadi tourism.[260] According to the German Federal Ministry of the Interior, the number of people who traveled to join the Islamic State had increased dramatically in early 2015, posing a direct threat to the nation-state. This new legislative Act followed an earlier Act in 2014 that granted authorities the power to revoke

---

[258] Counter-Terrorism and Security Act 2015, Schedule 3, paragraph 4.
[259] Counter-Terrorism and Security Act 2015, s 10.
[260] See http://www.dw.com/en/german-cabinet-approves-bill-to-stop-radicals-traveling-to-middle-east/a-18233282 accessed 15 February 2024.

or refuse an identity card for Islamic State supporters, which included the proscription of the Islamic State group and all activities in support in Germany. To comply with UN international norms, individuals who have been refused an identity card will instead be issued a substitute identity document stating 'not valid for travel outside of Germany.' As part of the risk management strategy inherent in the international and national response to the terrorist threat, some members of Germany's opposition party provided arguments similar to those raised by UK MPs during the enactment stages of the CTSA, stating that the powers are unconstitutional as they criminalize neutral behavior, as the moment of crime is far in advance of the actual crime.

Do we really need to be Criminalising Neutral Behaviour?

Since the introduction of the various bulk powers and decryption under the Investigatory Powers Act and the passing of the Online Safety Act 2023, legislative pre-emptive measures introduced will likely increase in use. In seeking to address potential terrorist threats, the storage of electronic communications data for 12 months and the bulk powers that enable such data to be analyzed by an algorithm have proven crucial in identifying potential threats within the ever-expanding volume of data. As technology advances and algorithms become more sophisticated, the utilisation of existing pre-emptive measures will be vital in thwarting terrorist attacks. However, granting such capabilities to the state has sparked scholarly discussions concerning mass surveillance, risk society, predictive policing, and the concept of 'pre-crime' measures.

Mass Data Surveillance

According to Ratcliffe *et al.*, citizens are subjected to mass surveillance in terms of CCTV camera use and its effects on crime reduction in the UK.[261] In terms of electronic communications data and Internet Connection Records that are retained for 12 months, and from the legal definition of surveillance under RIPA, such retention

---

[261] J. Ratcliffe, T. Taniguchi and R. B. Taylor (2009) The Crime Reduction Effects of Public CCTV Cameras: A Multi-Method Spatial Approach, *Justice Quarterly*, 26:4.

does not quite equate to mass surveillance. It would simply be impossible for UK law enforcement agencies to conduct surveillance on the entire data pool actively. The algorithmic screening of the stored electronic communications data means that most UK citizens' data would likewise not come under the remit.[262]

Risk Society: The resulting increase in state powers

The collection and storage of extensive data contribute significantly to the ongoing debate regarding the balance between collective security and individual privacy, fundamentally shaping risk management. For Beck, the term 'risk' is a modern concept that:

---

[262] I. Brown and D. Korff (2014) Foreign Surveillance: Law and Practice in a Global Digital Environment, *European Human Rights Law Review*, 3:243-251. See also A. S. Reid and N. Ryder (2010) For Whose Eyes Only? A Critique of the United Kingdom's Regulation of Investigatory Powers Act 2000, *Information and Communications Technology Law*, 10:2, 179-201.

'…inherently contains the concept of control…presumes decision making [and involves] talking about calculating the incalculable'.[263]

Beck's conceptualization in 2002 suggests that citizens may increasingly adopt a paranoid 'risk society' mentality as the international terror threat expands.[264] This link between prediction and risk, where the fear of a potential terrorist attack prompts an increase in state law enforcement capabilities, has arguably spurred the development of computer algorithms. These algorithms are designed to autonomously and rapidly sift through the vast amounts of stored data to identify potential threats. By linking prediction and risk, such algorithms search out the needles in the haystacks autonomously and quickly.[265] According to Furedi's analysis, 'fear plays a key role in twenty-first-century consciousness,' which has inevitably

---

[263] U. Beck (2002) The Terrorist Threat: World Risk Society Revisited, *Theory, Culture and Society*, 19:4, 39-55, 40.
[264] *Ibid.*
[265] *Ibid.* See also I. Kerr and J. Earle (2013) Prediction, Preemption, Presumption: How Big Data Threatens Big Picture Privacy, *Stanford Law Review Online*, available at https://www.stanfordlawreview.org/online/privacy-and-big-data-prediction-preemption-presumption/.

led to citizens' acceptance of increased state monitoring and, thereby, for Garland at least, control.[266] It is important to acknowledge that as citizens become more accustomed to state surveillance of stored data, driven by the risk society theory and technological advancements, the automated computer algorithms employed may become increasingly adept at sifting through the vast data, looking for potential terrorists. This evolution could lead to intelligence-led policing transitioning into a form of predictive-led policing.

Predictive Policing and Pre-Emptive Measures: Pre-crime

While the term predictive policing remains simply within the understanding of intelligence-led policing, it has nevertheless resulted in critics suggesting the UK is moving towards a 'pre-crime' scenario.[267] However, law

---

[266] F. Furedi (2007) The only thing we have to fear is the 'culture of fear' itself: How human thought and action are being stifled by a regime of uncertainty, available at http://frankfuredi.com/pdf/fearessay-20070404.pdf. See also D. Garland (2001) *The Culture of Control: Crime and social Order in Contemporary Society* (Oxford University Press).
[267] J. Richards (2016) *Needles in Haystacks: Law, Capability, Ethics, and Proportionality in Big Data Intelligence-*

enforcement cannot simply conduct surveillance or arrest without authorized legal powers and a specific identifiable criminal offense being committed. As such, the term 'pre-crime' does not exist legally. In fact, it is simply a fabricated term used by Hollywood in the movie 'Minority Report'. As discussed further below, collecting or disseminating terrorist-related data through the Internet is a criminal offense.[268] The same can be said for encouraging another to commit an act of terrorism. These are not pre-crime measures but pre-emptive criminal offenses aimed at preventing the would-be-terrorist from committing the physical act.

Following Beck's conceptualization above, pre-emptive measures are littered throughout the UK's legal counterterrorism structure simply because of the extraordinary terror threat.[269] As with the Investigatory Powers Act 2016, RIPA, and the CTSA, there has been a

---

Gathering, in A. Bunnik, A. Cawley, M. Mulqueen and A. Zwitter, *Big Data Challenges* (Palgrave Macmillan) p74. See also L. Zedner (2007) Pre-crime and post-criminology? *Theoretical Criminology*, 11:2.

[268] Terrorism Act 2000, ss 57, 58, and Terrorism Act 2006, ss 1, 2.

[269] *Supra* as per U. Beck (2002).

growing tendency and common theme to address anticipatory risk.[270] For Walker, these measures have habitually been reactive to the politics of the last atrocity.[271] In response, the UK has enacted certain provisions aimed at criminalizing the collection of terrorist material for terrorist purposes and at criminalizing the encouragement and dissemination of terrorist publications. Again, for Walker, the process of the radicalization of young Muslim men became a primary focus following the terrorist attack on London on the 7th of July 2005. In response to the gamut of ferociousness and the devastating nature of recent terrorist acts, early State intervention is essential before rather than after the attack.[272]

---

[270] C. Walker (2008) Terrorism: Terrorism Act 2000 s.57-direction to jury on defense of possession of items for defensive purposes, Case Comment, *Criminal Law Review* 72-80, 74.

[271] *Ibid.*

[272] For attack ion Turkey see http://edition.cnn.com/2016/03/13/world/ankara-park-blast/. For Ivory Coast attack see http://www.nytimes.com/2016/03/14/world/africa/gunmen-carry-out-fatal-attacks-at-resorts-in-ivory-coast.html?_r=0. For Northern Ireland terror attack see http://www.telegraph.co.uk/news/uknews/terrorism-in-the-uk/,

What are Statutory Preventative Measures? How do these fit with the definition of terrorism?

Statutory preventative measures form part of this anticipatory risk management approach, although enacted prior to Walker's point made above, and not in direct response to a terrorist attack. Under section 57 of the Terrorism Act 2000, if a person possesses an article in circumstances that give rise to a reasonable suspicion that such possession is for a purpose connected with the commission, preparation, or instigation of an act of terrorism, they commit an offense. Similarly, under section 58, a person commits an offense if they collect or make a record of information of a kind likely to be useful to a person committing or preparing an act of terrorism or if they possess a document or record containing information of that kind. This includes photographic and electronic communications data, both of which

---

and http://www.bbc.co.uk/news/northern_ireland. For Paris attack 2016 see: http://www.bbc.co.uk/news/world-europe-34818994 accessed 15 Feburary 2024.

increasingly become available to law enforcement by way of an Investigatory Powers authority.

Although section 58 introduces measures requiring less proof of intent than section 57, both are designed to allow for the early prosecution of the would-be-terrorist during the planning stages. Early intervention is the methodology here, rather than simply waiting for a suspect to commit the physical act planned. Also known as anticipatory offenses, these sections provide a correlative broad scope, meaning that more citizens are potentially brought under the scope of terrorist activity. As one might imagine, this has resulted in argumentation surrounding what exactly amounts to an article for the purposes of section 58.

In R v K, the UK Court of Appeal clarified that section 58 was not meant to criminalize the possession of theological or propagandist material and must provide practical assistance. The Court also emphasized that a document that merely encourages the commission of acts of terrorism does not fall within the definition, thus effectively limiting the scope of section 58.[273] A year later, in *R v G, R v J* the UK House of Lords (now UK Supreme Court) appeared to build upon this judgment, confirming that the defendant must be aware of the nature of the information contained in the article.[274] Ultimately, *J* argued an infringement of his European Convention on Human Rights Article 7 and 10 rights in the ECtHR, which failed.[275] According to Ackerman, this judicial interpretation strengthens the argument that the UK's counterterrorism legislation is overly broad and only tempered by the restraint of the judiciary, police, and Crown Prosecution Service (CPS), potentially justifying executive overreach.[276] Ackerman argues that the real threat to the public comes not from terrorism but from counterterrorism measures such as these.[277] Gearty raises similar concerns, noting that the Convention rights are

---

[273] [2008] EWCA Crim 185, [13].

[274] [2009] UKHL 13, [47]-[50].

[275] *Jobe v UK* [2011] 48278/09: echr Article 7 no punishment without law and Article 10 Freedom of Expression.

[276] B. Ackerman (2007) Before the Next Attack - Preserving Civil Liberties in an Age of Terrorism, *Public Law* 181-187.

[277] *Ibid.*

under 'severe attack from a variety of sources.'[278] According to Imran, what is now clear is that many 'of the questions raised in *K* may be rendered superfluous by the intervention of alternative provisions that reduce the necessity for reliance on section 58'.[279]

What is Inciting Terrorism? What is Encouragement?

A person commits an offense of incitement under section 59 of the Terrorism Act 2000 if they incite another to commit an act of terrorism, within or outside UK borders, if the act would constitute one of the following offenses:

1) Murder (contrary to UK Common Law);

2) An s18 offense of wounding with intent under the Offences Against the Person Act 1861;

3) Administering poison to a person under s23 Offences Against the Person Act 1861;

---

[278] C. Gearty (2007) Rethinking civil liberties in a counter-terrorism world, European Human Rights Law Review (2), 111-119.

[279] A. Imran (2011) Slaying the Monster: Sentencing, Criminal Law and Justice Weekly 175 JPN 151.

4) Damage to property endangering life, as under s1 Criminal Damage Act 1971.

The challenge here is that the incitement offense is limited to these four elements, and practically, it sets a high bar, making it quite challenging to establish. To bridge the gap between incitement and encouragement, thus lowering the threshold and enabling UK law enforcement to widen the scope of suspicion, sections 1 and 2 of the Terrorism Act 2006 might offer weight to Imran's reduction assessment and present even more 'expansive possibilities for the prosecution and conviction.'[280] Enacted as a result of the terrorist attack on London on 7th July 2005, and to reflect the provisions of Article 5 of the 2005 Council of Europe Convention on the Prevention of Terrorism, section 1 makes it an offense to encourage an act of terrorism, and section 2 makes it an offense to disseminate terrorist publications. Section 1 may have perhaps been enacted as a result of the earlier ruling in *R v K*.

---

[280] *Ibid.*

What is the Encouragement and Glorification of Terrorism?

Terrorism Act 2006

The Terrorism Act 2006 was aimed at criminalising 'speeches at meetings, sermons at places of worship, chants and placards at demonstrations, broadcasts and material posted on the Internet.'[281] A person will commit an offence of publishing a statement to directly encourage terrorism if:

(a) he publishes a statement or causes another to publish such a statement, and

---

[281] A. Jones QC, R. Bowers and H. D. Lodge (2006) *Blackstone's Guide to The Terrorism Act 2006*, (Oxford University Press) p.13.

(b) at the time he publishes it or causes it to be published, he

(c) intends members of the public to be directly or indirectly encouraged or otherwise induced by the statement to commit, prepare or instigate acts of terrorism or Convention offences; or

(d) is reckless as to such and

(e) the statement that is likely to be understood by some or all of the members of the public to whom it is published as a direct or indirect encouragement or other inducements to them to the commission, preparation or instigation of acts of terrorism or Convention offences.[282]

Jones *et al.* find that the concept of direct encouragement poses minimal challenges. The criminal act of publishing material with intent is akin to the offense of incitement under the Terrorism Act 2000. The offenses outlined in section 1 of the Terrorism Act 2006 can be committed with intent or recklessly, as to whether members of the public will be directly or indirectly

---

[282] Terrorism Act 2006, s 1(2)(b)(i)(ii).

encouraged or otherwise induced.[283] However, since this provision allows for indirect encouragement, its broad applicability is advantageous to law enforcement agencies in terms of scope.

Indirect Encouragement: Glorification

The glorification aspect was one of the most debated issues during the enactment of the Terrorism Act 2006 in the UK Parliament.[284] The primary concern revolved around the broad scope of the offense and its potential impact on civil liberties and human rights, particularly Article 10 of the European Convention on Human Rights, which guarantees freedom of expression. The Third Report of the Joint Committee on Human Rights in 2005 highlighted these concerns. While the Committee acknowledged the need for a new law, it also considered:

…that the offence of encouragement in clause 1 is not sufficiently legally certain to satisfy the requirement in Article 10 that interferences with freedom of expression

---

[283] Terrorism Act 2006, s 1(2)(b)(i) and (ii).

[284] *Supra* as per A. Jones QC, R. Bowers and H. D. Lodge (2006) p.13.

be "prescribed by law" because of (i) the vagueness of the glorification requirement, (ii) the breadth of the definition of "terrorism" and (iii) the lack of any requirement of intent to incite terrorism or likelihood of such offences being caused as ingredients of the offence.[285]

To ensure compliance with the European Convention on Human Rights (ECHR), the Committee recommended the removal of references to glorification, the insertion of a more precisely defined definition of terrorism, and the inclusion of an intent or subjective recklessness test to assess the likelihood of the provision.[286] It was also suggested that a reasonable excuse or public interest defence be added to further meet European Convention on Human Rights standards.[287] However, the Government rejected the amendments proposed by the House of Lords, and the then Labour Home Secretary Charles Clarke stated in Parliament that Section 1 of the

---

[285] Counter-Terrorism Policy and Human Rights: Terrorism Bill and related matters, House of Lords, House of Commons Joint Committee on Human Rights, Third Report of Session 2005–06, HL Paper 75-I HC 561-I, summary p.3.
[286] *Ibid.*
[287] *Ibid.*

Terrorism Act 2006 was intended to provide an exemplary description of what would constitute glorification.[288] Therefore, under Section 1, the statement must glorify the commission or preparation of terrorist attacks, including past, future, or in general terms, and it must be a statement that members of the public could reasonably be expected to infer that they should emulate the glorified conduct. Clarke, however, clarified that this description was not exhaustive.

Therefore, a statement that provides indirect encouragement is not limited to glorification. As part of the UK's preemptive approach, this section, coupled with section 5, creates a broader offense of preparing terrorist acts, which is closer to containing an offense of involvement, future intention, or even just espousal of the cause rather than the commission of an established crime.[289] It was argued this would appear to close off paths to enlightened discussion and debate utilising materials, as this could perceived as supporting acts of terrorism rather

---

[288] *Ibid.*
[289] *R v Rowe* [2008] Crim LR 72, see commentary.

than condemning it.[290] Given the gravity of the radicalisation problem, one can appreciate the political approach to the necessity of these powers. A similar approach is seen when looking at the dissemination of terrorist materials.

Dissemination of terrorist publications

Following section 2 of the Terrorism Act 2006, a person engages in conduct falling within if he distributes or circulates a terrorist publication, including the sale or lending of a publication, or the offering for sale or loan, or provides a service to others that enable the obtainment of the publication, including the transmission of the publication electronically. The offence of dissemination is completed if he intends his conduct to directly or indirectly encourage or provide assistance in the commission, preparation or instigation of acts of terrorism or is reckless as to such.[291] The Third Report of the Joint Committee on Human Rights raised the same concerns as those for the glorification of terrorism. They

---

[290] *Ibid.*
[291] Terrorism Act 2006 s 2(1).

argued this provision 'suffers from some of the same compatibility problems as those identified in relation to the proposed encouragement offence.'[292] This included 'the lack of connection to incitement to violence and the absence of any requirement that such incitement be either intended, carried out with reckless indifference, or likely.'[293] Again the Committee suggested a reasonable excuse or public interest clause be inserted, primarily aimed at providing a defence and protection for legitimate activities of the media and academics.[294] The requirement for this power, on balance, appears to be necessary given the amount of data disseminated through the Internet, within which section 3 of the Terrorism Act 2006 makes specific provision for the application of sections 1 and 2 to Internet activity, thereby preventing terrorist material from making its way onto the Internet and attempting to halt terrorist communication. As highlighted, the

---

[292] Counter-Terrorism Policy and Human Rights: Terrorism Bill and related matters, House of Lords, House of Commons Joint Committee on Human Rights, Third Report of Session 2005–06, HL Paper 75-I HC 561-I, summary pp.3-4.

[293] *Ibid.*

[294] *Ibid.*

enthused and encouraged would-be terrorists could potentially attempt to join terrorist groups fighting overseas.

Conclusion

In addition to the unquantifiable threat highlighted in the previous Chapter, this Chapter has illustrated the frustrated scenario fashioned by sudden increases in independent operational abilities. This has resulted in the introduction of pre-emptive legislative measures and a risk management style of policing. To this end the Chapter has highlighted the interconnection between the risk society theory and predictive policing.

Such pre-emptive measures include temporary travel restrictions and the criminalisation of neutral behaviour. Using a doctrinal approach, terms such as mass data surveillance and pre-crime measures have been discredited. Indeed, it would be physically impossible for law enforcement to conduct surveillance on the whole of the UK population's electronic communications data. It has further been shown that the term 'pre-crime' is simply a fabrication and misleadingly used, given that pre-emptive measures are in fact, criminal offences.

The requirements for pre-emptive measures have been evidenced throughout both the previous and this Chapter, in particular, highlighting that currently, counter-terrorism legislation fails to eliminate the terrorist groups' propaganda and terrorist-encrypted electronic communications data. Both of which play an integral part in increasing the security risks posed to the UK. It further fails to provide clarity in practical terms, given that the Terrorism Act 2006 appears to have undercut ss57 and 58 of the Terrorism Act 2000, where it could be argued the latter merely provides 'a useful side-arm.[295] Regardless, the balance between collective security and individual data privacy rights in the UK being fairly stable can be said for the pre-emptive legislative measures examined. Again this is because of the role and importance of judicial review, judicial independence, and the over-arching scrutiny provided by commissioners and parliamentary

---

[295] *Supra* as per A. Imran (2011).

committees. Since the passing of the Investigatory Powers Act 2016, an increase in the usage of these dedicated pre-emptive measures may serve to provide the state with positive outcomes.

Chapter Three: The Online Safety Act 2023: Inserting the last piece of the 'policing a risk society' jigsaw puzzle

Online Safety Act 2023

The responsibility of the state is to provide security for its citizens. Part of that responsibility is to ensure those citizens are as safe as possible from being radicalised online viewing extremist content that can lead to terrorist attacks. In providing such safety, the UK has introduced specialist counter-terrorism legislation criminalising actions, such as collecting data, providing for increased powers to law enforcement agencies, and ensuring there is a sufficient budget for those agencies to carry out investigations as effectively as possible. As we have discovered, the requirement for specialist legislation rests on the fact that conventional crime poses an indirect threat to the stability of the state, whereas terrorist activity poses a direct threat to that stability, is triadic in nature and ranges from actual disablement of state apparatus to a resultant feeling of insecurity amongst citizens. This has led to a risk-management approach to legislation and policing prowess built around risk-identification. Increased mass surveillance is the UK Government's answer in policing the risk society by assuming everyone is guilty until the risk profiles prove otherwise.

Since the Terrorism Act 2000, there have been no less than ten statutes, all dedicated to countering terrorism, and all, in some way or another, degrading human rights norms. In fact, Lord Hoffmann in *A and others v Secretary of State for the Home Department* put it rather eloquently when referring to control orders, suggesting that the real threat to the life of a nation comes not from terrorism but overly restrictive counter-terrorism laws.[296] In addition, there has been a significant increase in powers of

---

[296] [2004] UKHL 56 [97]

surveillance, with the enactment of the Investigatory Powers Act 2016, dedicated to countering the online proliferation of criminal activity. Since then, the discussion has evolved into the realms of more internet control measures, increased surveillance on electronic communications, and social media regulations aimed at making the internet experience safer.

Against the backdrop of online radicalisation and the use of the Internet by terrorists and extremists, the next point for this book is to discuss the form that regulatory measures of the Internet should take. Moving from other nation state's attempts at regulation, the chapter will analyse the Online Safety Act 2023 and discover whether it serves its purpose of regulation. The main issue of contention is that there appears to be no one-size-fits-all measure, given the diverse range of online illegal activity surrounding the many denotations of terrorism and extremism. With no internationally agreed definition of terrorism or extremism and no legal UK national definition of extremism, the risk assessments are left to the user-to-user provider and search service to implement risk assessments and for Ofcom to implement and enforce. On the one hand, content could be removed that is legitimately dangerous, and on the other hand, content could be removed that is not dangerous but rather thought provoking. Through all the borderline cases, we are bound to find constrictions on the freedom of expression, which is why laws of this nature have failed in other nation-states.

Particularly since the 7th July 2005 terrorist attack in London and the foiled attempted attack on the 21st July 2005, the UK Government has essentially increased, over time of course and usually in response to further successful attacks and potential threats identified, the Governance of Security. The latest of these is the Counter-Terrorism and Sentencing Act 2021, which increases sentencing for those convicted of terrorism-related offences. This was brought about after the terrorist attack in London carried out by Usman Khan, who was convicted for terrorism-related offences, and who claimed to have been rehabilitated. Powers afforded to law enforcement have also witnessed an expansion of surveillance measures, particularly by way of the Investigatory Powers Act 2016, which permits authorised bulk access to online communications. This book has evidenced the introduction of legislation that has moved from dealing with an attack to preventing and pre-empting terrorism. Thus, of course increasing the Governance of Security.

Despite the proliferation of laws and measures aimed at countering the threat, there remains the backdrop of the use of the Internet by terrorists and extremists in order to radicalise and recruit others to join their cause. This Chapter will highlight and evaluate the UK Government's Online Safety Act 2023, which aims to regulate online content and protect users from harmful material. The Act, introduced to the UK Parliament in May 2021, requires social media companies and other online platforms to take responsibility for the content on their sites and remove illegal or harmful content quickly. The Act has generated a lot of discussion and debate, including concerns about its potential impact on the freedom of expression, protected by Article 10 of the European Convention on Human Rights and Fundamental Freedoms 1950 (echr). While legitimately aimed at protecting people from harmful content, critics argue that the undefined use of this term could also lead to censorship and limit the free exchange of ideas online.

It is always worth highlighting the main issue the UK Government feels deserving of specialist legislation first. To achieve this, the chapter will discuss a recent terrorism case study that was before the UK courts.

Think back to the case study we discussed in the first Chapter, remember the young boy who was essentially groomed online, whilst at home. Ask yourselves: is this young boy a terrorist? An extremist? Or merely a victim of online professional grooming and manipulation? Should the state have a duty to protect vulnerable children online from exploitation, grooming, and radicalisation in this way?

The online universe is gargantuan. For the oldies such as myself, the size and speed of the 21st-century Internet is simply unfathomable.

The Internet in 2024

The internet is continually growing, and people are using social platforms at lightning speed. Statistics show that in 2022, within every 60 seconds there were;

- 694 million songs streamed in the USA alone.

- 231 million emails sent.

- 167 million videos watched on TikTok.

- 44 million people viewing Facebook live streams.

- 6 million people online shopping.

- 5.9 million Google searches.[297]

Despite calculating this data since 2016, the methodology used to gather this data remains unknown.[298] However, accepted as accurate by many experts, including Kemp, statistics showed that in 2020, 4.54 billion people used the Internet, 5.12 billion use mobile phones, with 3.8 billion using social media.[299] More and more people are using the Internet at home and on the go, via smart

---

[297] H. Patel, 'What happens in an internet minute', Bond High Plus, available at https://www.bondhighplus.com/2022/01/08/what-happen-in-an-internet-minute/ (Last visited 11 April 2023).

[298] S. Hale-Ross, 'The Investigatory Powers Act 2019: The Human Rights Conformist', in S. Hale-Ross and D. Lowe Eds, Terrorism and State Surveillance of Communications (Routledge, 2019) p68.

[299] S. Kemp 'Digital 2020: 3.8 Billion People use Social Media' Special Report, at https://wearesocial.com/blog/2020/01/digital-2020-3-8-billion-people-use-social-media (last viewed 13 April 2023).

devices. The freedom this presents citizens with, in terms of expressing opinions and beliefs that can potentially reach millions in a matter of minutes, is extraordinary. Societal ideas, political opinions and cultural beliefs essentially form the Internet, and especially open-sourced social media, such as Facebook and X.[300] As with all legitimate technological growth, what often follows is criminal exploitation, or in our case, terrorist exploitation. This was perhaps no better emphasised than by the Christchurch terrorist attacks, which were live-streamed through Facebook by the terrorists. The clips were still available to view on platforms some six months after the event. This inability to take down the content quickly highlighted the Achilles heel of such platforms when faced with the live and viral dissemination of extremely violent content.

---

[300] Statistica, (2018) 'The Statistics Portal, Global digital population as of October 2018', Statistica website, at https://www.statista.com/statistics/617136/digital-population-worldwide/ (last viewed 12 April 2023).

The Internet is the key technology for terrorists.[301] Used expertly by Al-Qaeda, and, more recently, by the Islamic State and other terrorist organisations such as National Action in the UK. They provide grooming and recruitment tools, online marketing, and advertising to spread the political and ideological message.[302] Al Qaeda advocated spreading rumours and statements in their operational manual, which outlined the 20-year strategic plan 2001-2020. In *Queen v Said Namouth*, the Court of Québec highlighted several messaging characteristics of Islamist terrorist groups, such as publicising speeches given by leaders of Al-Qaeda; inciting others to commit terrorist action; urging support for mainstream and affiliated groups; providing advice on computer security and hacking; and the conduction of psychological warfare

---

[301] M. Rudner, 'Electronic Jihad: The Internet as Al Qaeda's Catalyst for Global Terror' (2017*) Studies in Conflict & Terrorism* 40:1, 10-23, 10.

[302] *Ibid.* See also S. Hale-Ross, '*Digital Privacy, Terrorism and Law Enforcement: The UK's Response to Terrorist Communication*' (Routledge, 2019) pp44-47.

and publishing magazines like *Inspire* and *Sawt al-Jihad* (the Voice of Jihad).[303]

For Hoffman, Internet communications are used by terrorist organisations in a constructed and contextualised way to address specific objectives.[304] More recently, social media, chat rooms and online gaming have been the preferred method when terrorist groups, such as the Islamic State, have been focused on recruitment.[305] The power wielded by social media and the spread of information becomes a problem if an extremist group that advocates violence uses this to contact and radicalise

---

[303] Court of Québec, District of Montreal, Criminal and Penal Division, H.M. *The Queen v Said Namouh*, No. 500-73-002831-077 and 500-73-002965-081, 1 October 2009. The individual concerned, Said Namouh, was convicted of terrorism offenses under Canada's Anti-Terrorism Act 2001. For more information on *Sawt al-Jihad*, see n 2 above, p46.

[304] B. Hoffman, '*Inside Terrorism*' (Columbia University Press, 2006) p. 199.

[305] No 2 above, p51

young and vulnerable people. Social media and the Internet have been an absolute gift for terrorist groups such as the Islamic State.[306] The Islamic State used this expertly, having an organisational structure similar to a private corporate business, where a whole separate department was formed to handle online advertising.[307]

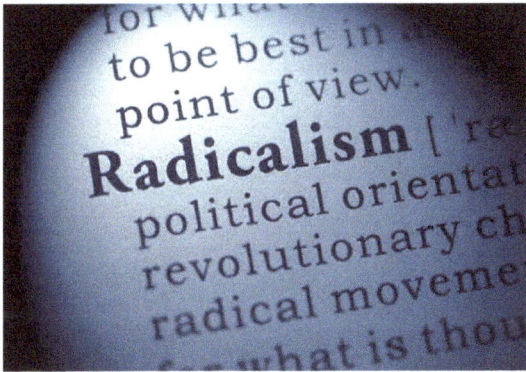

Recruitment of young people and adults with learning disabilities is especially concerning given the level of vulnerability within this group. A study by Caton and Landman in 2020 illustrated the growth in smartphone

---

[306] J. Klausen (2015) 'Tweeting the Jihad: Social Media Networks of Western Foreign Fighters in Syria and Iraq', *Studies in Conflict & Terrorism*, 39(1), 1–22, 3.

[307] H. J. Ingram (2015a) 'The Strategic Logic of Islamic State Information Operations', *Australian Journal of International Affairs*, 69(6), 729–752, p.732.

and tablet use amongst this group that convolutes the challenging balance of risks and benefits, of online safety and freedoms.[308] Within this framework, the study reinforces the fact that online radicalisation and grooming for terrorism follows the same pattern associated with sexual predators. As highlighted in the case study, in this way, the groomer intentionally and slowly develops emotional links to gain the trust of the victim, which then often escalates to manipulation and reinforcement of the message being impressed. In response, the UK Government released a White Paper dealing with online harms, which of course, has now accumulated into the Online Safety Act 2023.[309]

---

[308] S. Caton, R. Landman, 'Internet Safety, Online Radicalisation and Young People with Learning Disabilities' (2021) *British Journal of Learning Disabilities*, 1-10, 2. See also Ofcom, 'Online Nation: Narrative Report' (2020) at https://www.ofcom.org.uk/research-and-data/internet-and-on-demand-research/online-nation/narrative (last visited 12 April 2024).

[309] HM Government, 'Online Harms' (2020) Command Paper Number 354, at https://www.gov.uk/government/consultations/online-harms-white-paper/outcome/online-harms-white-paper-full-government-response#executive-summary (last visited 12 April 2023).

The Case for Regulation

The case for robust regulatory action grows year on year, and according to the UK government's findings, this is likely to increase. They found:

In terms of illegal content and activity, there were more than 69 million images and videos related to child sexual exploitation and abuse referred by US technology companies to the National Centre for Missing and Exploited Children in 2019,[310] an increase of more than 50% on the previous year.[311] In 2019, of the over 260,000 reports assessed by the Internet Watch Foundation, 132,730 contained images and/or videos of children being sexually abused (compared to 105,047 in 2018), and 46% of reports involved imagery depicting children who appeared to be 10 years old or younger.[312] Between its

---

[310] See https://www.missingkids.org/gethelpnow/cybertipline (last visited 12 April 2023).

[311] See https://www.nytimes.com/2020/02/07/us/online-child-sexual-abuse.html (last visited 12 April 2023).

[312] The Internet Watch Foundation Annual Report 2019, at https://www.iwf.org.uk/sites/default/files/reports/2020-04/IWF_Annual_Report_2020_Low-res-Digital_AW_6mb.pdf (last visited 12 April 2023).

launch in January 2015 and March 2019, 8.3 million images have been added to the Child Abuse Image Database.[313]

The findings show that terrorist material and propaganda, designed to radicalise, recruit and inspire, continue to present a unique set of somewhat qualifiable elements. This taken in conjunction with the gargantuan scale of the internet, essentially accumulates to bring an unquantifiable risk. The security risks posed to the UK emanate from three main sources being: Islamist ideologies, far-right extremism, and single-issue threats

---

[313] Office for National Statistics, January 2020, at https://www.ons.gov.uk/peoplepopulationandcommunity/crimean djustice/datasets/childsexualabuseappendixtables (last visited 12 April 2023). See n 7 above, paragraph 8.

such as those who subscribe to movements that fall below counter-terrorism legislative capture.

The Involuntary-celibate movement, shortened to 'Incel', and the QAnon movements would fall within this category. Considering these movements do not conform to an organisational structure, they remain difficult for the UK Government to proscribe. As a movement, they would be simply deemed as an extremist ideology and, therefore fall below counter-terrorism legislative capture. Compounding this issue of course, is the lack of an objective, legal definition of extremism.

The Security Threats facing the UK.

Single-Issue: Incels

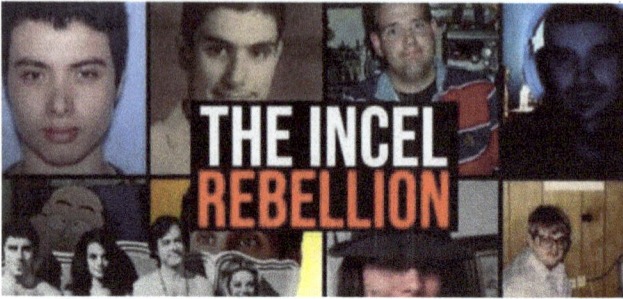

Initially set up in the late 1990s as a support cluster for single people who could not find a partner, the movement now represents one of the most dangerous subcultures on the Internet.[314] Although not an actual organisation or group per se, the Incel movement, which advocates serious violence towards what they term as 'Chads' and 'Stacys', has been able to use online platforms to spread and share the ideology.[315] This movement reached public

---

[314] J. Taylor, 'The Woman Who Founded the 'Incel' Movement', BBC News, 30 August 2018, at https://www.bbc.co.uk/news/world-us-canada-45284455 (last visited 12 April 2023). See Also https://www.vox.com/the-highlight/2019/4/16/18287446/incel-definition-reddit (last visited 12 April 2023).

[315] R. van der Veer, 'Analysing Personal Accounts of Perpetrators of Incel Violence: What do they want and who do they target'? International Centre for Counter-Terrorism, The Hague

news in the US in 2014, when Eliot Rodger killed six people, injured 14 others, and then killed himself after leaving his 107,000-word manifesto. He also posted a video clip on YouTube called Eliot Rodgers Retribution, where he essentially complained about being rejected by women, explaining his attack's plan and motives behind it. Since then, there has been an attack in Canada in 2018 by Alex Minassian, and a failed attack in the US in 2020, both of whom claimed to have been inspired by the Incel movement and their martyr, Rodgers.[316] Despite being

---

(2020) at https://icct.nl/publication/analysing-personal-accounts-of-perpetrators-of-incel-violence-what-do-they-want-and-who-do-they-target/ (last visited 12 April 2023).

[316] A. Bhattacharya, 'Canada's first: Teen INCEL who killed a woman charged with terrorism', Hindustan Times, 20 May 2020 at https://www.hindustantimes.com/world-news/canada-s-first-teen-incel-who-killed-a-woman-charged-with-terrorism/story-ZuqyHhBIoyM4bQssw5KXAL.html (last visited 12 April 2023). See also A. Court, 'Involuntary Celibate man, 23, accidentally amputated his own hand making a bomb to blow up hot cheerleaders', The Daily Mail, 6 June 2020 at https://www.dailymail.co.uk/news/article-8393947/Man-

charged with a terrorist offence, the Incel movement is largely considered to remain outside the ambit of terrorism.[317] Largely this means that online conversations on blogs, such as the 'inceloshere' and 'manosphere', are less monitored by law enforcement.[318]

A growing Incel presence is currently expanding within these online spaces provided by the Internet and the Darknet, where it is estimated that up to 2000 men in the UK label themselves as such.[319] The emerging risks are clear from three referrals made to the UK's Prevent

---

amputates-hand-making-bomb-designed-blow-hot-cheerleaders.html (last visited 12 April 2023).

[317] S. Bell, 'Despite Crackdown on Incels, Their Discussion Forums are Still Online', Global News, 9 June 2020 at https://globalnews.ca/news/7022100/incel-discussion-forums-still-online-crackdown/ (last visited 12 April 2023).

[318] The 'inceloshere' follows the ecosystem approach to studying extremist online spaces, and hosting spaces such as sub-Reddits, online forums, Instagram, WhatsApp and Telegram are best understood as working together in sync, as a dynamic network which is collectively known as the 'inceloshere'.

[319] M. Evans, 'Counter-terrorism Police Investigate Potential Threat Posed by Violent Incels', The Telegraph, 6 March 2020 at https://www.telegraph.co.uk/news/2020/03/06/counter-terrorism-police-investigate-potential-threat-posed/ (last visited 12 April 2023).

Scheme in March 2021 to 77 cases by March 2022.[320] According to reports in 2022, approximately 1000 references to misogyny or violent action have been recorded daily, predominantly taking place in the 'inceloshere'.[321] From April 2022 to the year ending 31 March 2023, 6,817 people were referred to Prevent under the UK's counter-terrorism strategy CONTEST. Although individuals aged 15 to 20 represent the largest proportion, additionally 2,628 were between 11 and 15 years old, and perhaps even more concerning is that 256 referrals were made for those under 10 years of age.[322]

---

[320] V. Dodd, 'Large rise in men referred to Prevent over women-hating incel ideology', The Guardian, 26 January 2023 at https://www.theguardian.com/uk-news/2023/jan/26/large-rise-in-men-referred-to-prevent-over-women-hating-incel-ideology (last visited 12 April 2023).

[321] M. Townsend, 'Experts fear rising global 'incel' culture could provoke terrorism', The Telegraph, 30 October 2022 at https://www.theguardian.com/society/2022/oct/30/global-incel-culture-terrorism-misogyny-violent-action-forums (last visited 12 April 2023).

[322] HM Government, Home Office Official Statistics, 'Individuals referred to and supported through the Prevent Programme, April 2022 to March 2023', England and Wales, 14 December 2023, at https://www.gov.uk/government/statistics/individuals-referred-to-prevent/individuals-referred-to-and-supported-through-the-prevent-programme-april-2022-to-march-

Statistics appear to indicate a further growth in the Incel threat, arguably brought about by the increase in support for misogynistic online influences.[323] Influencers' stylistic framing of Incel content, particularly on TikTok, presents a real danger and challenge to security. This stylistic approach employs covert terminology and language, emotional appeals that attempt to legitimise ingrained misconceptions of male victimhood and female privilege, and a further attempt at the normalisation of stereotypes.[324] This Incel movement, which sits within the manosphere online community, shares grievances and works together to formulate solutions. Incel solutions include but are not limited to, Government mandated girlfriends; rape which often involves torture; the murder of women by means of mass shootings; paedophilia,

---

2023#:~:text=this%20statistical%20release.-,Key%20results,on%20(2015%2F16) accessed 27 January 2024.

[323] S. McCullough, 'Online misogyny: the "manosphere". Extremist digital sexism with dangerous real-world consequences'. The Canadian Museum for Human Rights, 2023, at https://humanrights.ca/story/online-misogyny-manosphere (last visited 17 January 2023).

[324] A. I. Solea and L. Sugiura. 'Mainstreaming the Blackpill: Understanding the Incel Community on TikTok'. European Journal on Criminal Policy Research, 2023, 29, 311–336.

where children aged 12 are described as being 'in their prime'; Human Growth Hormone and the ideas of having leg extension surgery and facial surgery; and 'Black-Pill' suicide.[325] Members of this community often groom others by offering answers to the secrets of life and being an adolescent and help in dealing with being involuntary celibate.

Whilst this movement is not classed as terrorist, one can certainly appreciate that such an attack inspired by it would be classed as single-issue terrorism. According to the Europol Terrorism Situation and Trend Report in 2019, Jihadist, left-wing and right-wing inspired terrorism remains the largest threat to the European Union. Single-issue terrorism is said to come predominantly from animal rights and environmentalism.[326] In fact, there is no mention whatsoever of the Incel movement. This could perhaps simply be due to the fact the European Union has

---

[325] n 21 above

[326] European Union, Europol, Terrorism Situation and Trend Report 2019, at https://www.europol.europa.eu/tesat-report (last visited 12 April 2024).

not yet suffered from an Incel-inspired attack, and the number of inspired attacks remains low across the globe.

The Irish Republican Army

The 'Troubles' have certainly been well documented and those interested in this would be wise to read the work provided by Peter Taylor. This Chapter, however, moves past the Troubles and starts with a focus on the Real Irish Republican Army (RIRA) and 32 County Sovereignty Movement (CSM). During a bitter conflict and towards the end of the Troubles, a political solution was sought by both Nationalist Organisations and Republican Groups, resulting in the Good Friday Agreement in 1998. At his time, the Provisional Irish Republican Army (PIRA) called a ceasefire, along with some Unionist groups, but this resulted in the formation of an IRA splinter group called the Real IRA and Continuity IRA. A prominent figure during this time, Martin McGuiness, essentially moved from terrorist to politician as he helped Gerry Adams lead Sinn Fein in the Good Friday Agreement.

They say a picture speaks a thousand words, and this one certainly does, as these two men here from left to right, Rev Ian Paisley (Democratic Unions Party) and Martin McGuiness (Sinn Fein), were bitter enemies during the Troubles.

The Real IRA

Republican and Unionist groups that continue to fight to this day find the above picture extremely hard to digest, as they still feel the bitterness. The Real IRA members felt that after fighting the British for thirty years, both the Provisional IRA and its political wing, Sinn Fein (led by Gerry Adams), had betrayed them and the cause of fighting for a united Ireland (Northern Ireland comprising six counties) and the removal of the British out of Northern Ireland. The declaration in this picture here clearly shows the Real IRA clubbing together the Police

ÓGLAIGH NA hÉIREANN

THE REAL IRA

*ANYONE WHO COMES TO OUR ATTENTION REGARDING PASSING ON OF INFORMATION TO THE PSNI,GARDAI, MI5 OR SINN FÉIN WILL BE DEALT WITH IN THE APPROPRIATE MANNER.

*ANYONE INVOLVED IN DEALING AND/OR SELLING OF DRUGS WIL NOT BE TOLERATED BY YOUR LOCAL BRIGADE.

*IN REGARDS TO ANTI-SOCIAL BEHAVOUR IN OUR AREA,IT WILL BE ELIMINATED IN DUE COURSE.

THE TRUE SOLDIERS OF IRELAND

Service of Northern Ireland (PSNI) that replaced the old Royal Ulster Constabulary (RUC), and MI5 (the British Security Service) with Sinn Fein.

One of the first responses by the Real IRA to the Good Friday agreement was the bombing of Omagh in County Tyrone in 1998, resulting in 29 deaths and 220 people injured. The car bomb was in the red car on your top left, and then what followed was the devastation captured in the picture below.

The New IRA

In August 2012, the Real IRA joined with Republicans Against Anti-Social Behaviour and Drugs (RAAD), which was made up of former members of the Provisional IRA and disaffected former members, to form a New IRA faction, simply called the IRA. Two events in November 2012 signaled their intent. First was the killing of a prison officer, David Black, who worked at Mughaberry Prison in November 2012. Second was the finding of bombs believed to be used to booby-trap cars in Ballymagrry Lane in Belfast.

Saoradh was formed in 2016 and shortly after released the following statement:

- Today, Saturday the 24th of September 2016, we, a significant collective of Irish Republican activists, who for a number of years have acted autonomously, have, after a number of years of debate, consultation and organisation today in Ard Fheis organised, constituted and launched a Revolutionary Irish Republican Party, the Party's name is Saoradh.

- Saoradh believes that the Irish People should govern Ireland with wealth-producing mechanisms in the ownership of the Irish People. This cannot happen while British imperialism undemocratically retains control of Irish destinies and partitions our nation, this cannot happen while a neo-colonial elite in a subservient supposed indigenous administration sells the nation's labour and natural resources to international capital.

- Saoradh does not believe that British imperialism or capitalist exploitation can be confronted in the structures they have created to consolidate their undemocratic control of the Irish nation. As such we believe any assembly claiming to speak for the Irish People without being elected by the united people of the Irish nation to be illegal.

- Saoradh will seek to organise and work with the Irish People rather than be consumed and usurped by the structures of Ireland's [enemies]. Standing on a long and proud revolutionary Irish Republican history of resistance, inspired by the actions and words of Tone of Connolly, of Mellows, of Costello and of Sands, upholding the founding documents of our forefathers – the 1916 proclamation, the Declaration of Independence and the democratic programme of the first Dáil, Saoradh hereby declares its commitment to the unfinished revolution, the liberation of Ireland and the social emancipation of the Irish People.

The New IRA and Saoradh represent a significant threat to the stability of Northern Ireland, as assessed by the Security Service to be 'severe'. Despite the fact that the PSNI and Gardai have managed to prevent planned attacks with the use of intelligence and informants, there are members of the new IRA who remain unknown. The PSNI and Gardai believe that some of the members of the IRA are experienced former Provisionals that can manage and organise the IRA into battalions with a strong and cohesive brigade leadership. Having experienced former Provisionals in their ranks it is feared the IRA will find out current informants and deal with them, causing fear, and, not knowing what current activities are planned, dissident attacks could spread throughout the Province and onto the British mainland.

As Gerry Adams (the then president of Sinn Fein) said following the Omagh bombing by the Real IRA in 1998, 'They've not gone away, you know.' And how right he was. During 10-14 February 2014, the IRA claimed responsibility for a series of parcel bombs sent to army recruitment offices in Oxford, Brighton, Canterbury, Slough, Aldershot, Reading and Chatham. Then, on 18 April 2019, investigative journalist Lyra McKee was murdered while observing rioting in the Creggan district of Derry. Mobile phone footage was released showing a masked gunman opening fire with a handgun. Saoradh subsequently released a statement attributing the shooting to 'a republican volunteer [that] attempted to defend people from the PSNI/RUC', after an incursion by heavily armed crown forces claiming that McKee was killed accidentally. Some recent incidents include:

- On 19 April 2021, a bomb was left near a police officer's car outside her home in County Londonderry in an attempt to kill her and her young daughter. Police said they linked the attempted murder to the New IRA.

- On 18 April 2022, Police Officers were attacked with petrol bombs following an Easter parade linked to dissident republicans in Derry. The police described the attack at the City Cemetery on 18 April as premeditated. The violence broke out following a parade that had been planned by the National Republican Commemoration Committee, which organises events on behalf of Saoradh.

- A police patrol vehicle was damaged in a bomb attack in Strabane, County Tyrone, on 17 November 2022. Police said a strong line of inquiry was that the dissident republican group, the New IRA, was behind the attack. Four men who were arrested were later released.

- On 20 November 2022, a delivery driver was held at gunpoint by a number of men and forced to abandon his car outside Waterside police station in Londonderry. A suspicious device, which was later described by police as an elaborate hoax, was placed in the vehicle. Chief Super Intendent Nigel Goddard described the attack as 'reckless' and said detectives believed the New IRA was involved.

- Senior police officer Detective Chief Inspector John Caldwell was shot at a sports complex in Omagh, County Tyrone, on 22 February 2023. He was off duty and was putting footballs into the boot of his car after coaching young people when two gunmen approached him and shot him several times. An attempted murder investigation was launched. Police said the primary focus of their investigation was on violent dissident republicans, including the New IRA. The New IRA later claimed responsibility in a typed statement that appeared in Londonderry on Sunday, 26 February.

- In March 2023, the terrorism threat level in Northern Ireland was increased from substantial to severe, meaning the risk of attack or attacks is now "highly likely" instead of "likely". Based on an MI5 intelligence assessment, the move reverses a downgrade to the threat level in 2022, the first such downgrade in 12 years. A severe threat level is one step below critical, the highest level of threat. Of course, this came after the shooting of Detective Chief Inspector John Caldwell in February 2023 and a bomb attack on police officers in November 2022.

- In April 2023, a petrol bomb attack on officers followed an illegal republican parade in Londonderry and came on the eve of a visit by USA President Joe Biden to Belfast.

- In August 2023, a list containing the details of 10,000 police officers and civilian staff was reported to be in the hands of dissident republicans. The information was contained in a spreadsheet mistakenly released as part of a PSNI response to a freedom of information request. Chief Constable Simon Byrne said the data breach was on an industrial scale and included the surnames, initials and ranks of colleagues. He said dissident republicans could use the information, part of which appeared in redacted form on a wall in west Belfast, to 'intimidate or target officers and staff.'

Since then in January 2024, it was reported that the New IRA have threatened to target security forces, including police, prison officers and other civil service members.[327] It remains to be seen if the New IRA have the capability to launch an attack on mainland Britain, emulating the PIRA in the earlier days.

Loyalist terror groups have also not fully disappeared, and neither has support for them. In November 2013 it was reported that the UVF ceasefire was called off. Recent attacks include:

- On 4 March 2021, the Ulster Defence Association (UDA), Ulster Volunteer Force (UVF), and Red Hand Commando renounced their current participation in

---

[327] N. Campbell (2024) Terror group condemned as 'death cult' after 'New IRA' threat to target security forces in 2024, Belfast   Telegraph   at https://www.belfasttelegraph.co.uk/news/northern-ireland/terror-group-condemned-as-death-cult-after-new-ira-threat-to-target-security-forces-in-2024/a767089543.html accessed 19 February 2024.

the Good Friday Agreement in a letter to (the then) Prime Minister Boris Johnson.

- On 11 April 2021, following a week of rioting in Loyalist communities, the UVF reportedly orders the removal of Catholic families from a housing estate in Carrickfergus.

- On 1 November 2021, a bus was hijacked and burnt by armed men on Abbot Drive in Newtownards, County Down. Police blamed a local faction of the UVF.

- On 25 March 2022, the UVF was blamed for a proxy bomb attack targeting a peace-building event in Belfast, where Irish Foreign Minister Simon Coveney was speaking. Armed men hijacked a van on the Shankill Road, Belfast and forced the driver to take a device to a church on the Crumlin Road.

- On 26 March 2022, the UVF was linked to a hoax bomb alert at a bar in Warrenpoint, County Down.

Far-Right Wing Extremism

Far-right wing extremism remains one of the largest concerns facing counter-terrorism law enforcement in the UK, despite being the first Western state to proscribe far-right organisations, such as National Action.

National Action

National Action is essentially a far-right neo-Nazi terrorist organisation, which was founded in 2013 by Alex Davies, who has now been subsequently jailed for 8 and half years. The leader was Chris Lythgoe, who since July 2018 has also been serving his time at His Majesty's pleasure and held its headquarters in Warrington, Cheshire, UK. They were reasonably well organised, essentially bringing together other like-minded factions to join a wider cause. Following proscription (meaning Banning by the UK Government), in November 2017, six people; 31-year-old Christopher Lythgoe, from Warrington; Garron Helm, 24, of Seaforth, Merseyside; Matthew Hankinson, 23, of Newton-le-Willows, Merseyside; and Andrew Clarke, 33, and Michael Trubini, 35, both of Warrington, along with Jack Renshaw, were charged with being members of National Action. Two of the men, Lythgoe and Renshaw, were also charged with being involved in a plot to murder the West Lancashire MP Rosie Cooper with a machete and of threatening to kill a police officer. In July 2017, a former National Action member, Robbie Mullen, reported the plot to the anti-racism organisation Hope Not Hate, who reported the matter to the police. In June 2018, at the Old Bailey in London, Renshaw pleaded guilty to plotting to murder Rosie Cooper and to threatening to kill a police officer. The following month, Hankinson and Lythgoe were found guilty of being members of National Action and jailed for six years and eight years, respectively.

Further arrests and charges were brought in May 2018, where the 'poster boy', Wayne Bell, was found guilty of membership and sentenced to 4 years custodial. And in March 2020, four people were convicted of membership and sentenced to between 3 and 5 years. In October and November 2018, a number of other members were convicted, including Adam Thomas, 22, who was found guilty under s11 Terrorism Act 2000 and s58 Terrorism Act 2000. Adam was vilified in the UK press for naming his child 'Adolf'.

Right-wing related attacks in the UK include the Murder/assassination of MP Jo Cox on 16 June 2016 by Thomas Mair, a 52-year-old white nationalist, who shot and stabbed the MP outside a surgery in Birstall, West Yorkshire, and severely wounded a passer-by who came to her aid. The attack was treated as an act of terrorism, and in sentencing Mair to life imprisonment, the judge said, 'There is no doubt that this murder was done for the purpose of advancing a political, racial and ideological cause, namely that of violent white supremacism and exclusive nationalism most associated with Nazism and its modern forms'.

On 19 June 2017, we saw the Finsbury Park Attack, where Darren Osborne, a 47-year-old British man, drove a van into Muslim worshippers near Finsbury Park Mosque, London. On 23 June, Osborne was charged with terrorism-related murder and attempted murder. In February 2018, at Woolwich Crown Court, he was found guilty of Murder and Attempted Murder and was sentenced to life imprisonment. Then, in February 2018, Ethan Stables, a white supremacist, was arrested after plotting a machete attack in an LGBTQ+ parade.

Regarding far-right extremism, during 2021-2022, and then again 2022-2023, Prevent has seen a 30% increase year on year in referrals made overall, with individuals aged between 15 to 20 accounting for the largest proportion.[328] Figures highlight that 20% was extreme

---

[328] HM Government, Home Office Official Statistics, 'Individuals referred to and supported through the Prevent Programme, April 2021 to March 2022', England and Wales, 26 January 2023 at https://www.gov.uk/government/statistics/individuals-referred-to-and-supported-through-the-prevent-programme-april-2021-to-march-2022/individuals-referred-to-and-supported-through-the-prevent-programme-april-2021-to-march-2022#:~:text=In%20the%20year%20ending%20March%202022%2C%20there%20were%206%2C406%20referrals,the%20spread%20of%20COVID%2D19. (last visited 12 January 2024). See also HM Government, Home Office Official Statistics, 'Individuals referred to and supported through the Prevent Programme, April 2022 to March 2023', England and Wales, 14 December 2023, at

right-wing related, followed by 2% for Islamist radicalisation.[329] The 2022 report then confirmed that from 2020 to 2021, the number of extreme right-wing referrals continues to outpace the Islamist related, as do the Channel adoption cases.[330] Since the enactment of the Counter-Terrorism and Security Act 2015 (CTSA) which placed a legal duty on schools, universities, and other public institutions to prevent people from being drawn into terrorism, referrals have continued to increase.

The Islamist Threat

Despite a year-on-year reduction in Prevent referrals for Islamist ideological extremism and terrorism, the threat remains.[331] According to the UK's Security Service (MI5), the threat, which falls within the ambit of international terrorism set by the Joint Terrorism Analysis

---

https://www.gov.uk/government/statistics/individuals-referred-to-prevent/individuals-referred-to-and-supported-through-the-prevent-programme-april-2022-to-march-2023#:~:text=this%20statistical%20release.-,Key%20results,on%20(2015%2F16) accessed 27 January 2024.

[329] *Ibid.*

[330] *Ibid.*

[331] *Ibid.*

Centre, is currently assessed to be substantial.[332] This means that an attack is *likely*.

Case Study: The Islamic State

The Islamic State terrorist group appeared to come from nowhere and spread across Syria and Iraq at incredible speed.[333] The origin of the Islamic State dates back to the Second Iraq War in the early 2000s, founded

---

[332] See Threat Levels | MI5 - The Security Service (last visited 28 January 2024). See also Joint Terrorism Analysis Centre | MI5 - The Security Service (last visited 28 January 2024).

[333] D. Byman (2015) Al Qaeda, The Islamic State and the Global Jihadist Movement, (Oxford University Press) pp.166-167. See also M. W. Nance (2015) The Terrorists of Iraq: Inside the Strategy and Tactics of the Iraqi Insurgency 2003-2014, (CRC Press) pp.297-300.

by Abu Musab al-Zarqawi in 2004. Originally, the group was called Islamic State in Iraq, and the group became an umbrella organisation under Al-Qaeda in Iraq in 2006.[334] In 2010, the leadership was transferred to Awwad Ibrahim Ali al-Badri al-Samarrai, also known as al-Baghdadi, who went on to rebuild military capabilities. Within three years, the group was carrying out terrorist attacks in the local region.[335] In an attempt to legitimise the Islamic State and solidify its existence and presence in the region and beyond, al-Samarrai took the name Abu Bakr al-Baghdadi. In April of that same year, the Islamic State merged with other groups to create the Islamic State in Iraq and the Levant/al-Sham (ISIL/ISIS).[336] Taking advantage of significant political unrest in the region, ISIL/ISIS grew

---

[334] See http://www.bbc.co.uk/news/world-middle-east-29052144 accessed 27 January 2024.

[335] *Supra* as per Byman at pp.306-308.

[336] Abu Bakr is an infamous name within the Islamic religion, being the name of the prophet Muhammad's father-in-law and chief adviser, becoming a caliph. This name resonates with Muslims and deep within the Muslim psychology, and was therefore chosen very carefully. For further information see P Mosendz (2014) How the head of ISIS got his name: Abu Bakr al-Baghdadi chose a name with historic resonance in the Muslim world, Europe Newsweek, http://europe.newsweek.com/abu-bakr-al-baghdadi-abu-dua-invisible-sheikh-awwad-ibrahim-ali-al-badri-al-282939?rm=eu accessed 27 January 2024.

exponentially, taking control of various villages, towns and cities. By 2014, the group had accumulated a lot of ground with the proclamation of a Caliphate, becoming known thereafter as the Islamic State. Abu Mosa was appointed as the head press officer, and in June 2014, they released a press statement stating:

...the Islamic State has been established. And we will not stop. Don't be cowards and attack us with drones. Instead, send your soldiers, the ones we humiliated in Iraq. We will humiliate them everywhere, God willing, and we will raise the flag of Allah in the White House.[337]

During this time, the Islamic State realised that it needed more resources, particularly new fighters who would be willing to die for the cause. To plug the gap in the number of fighters, a professional and business-like press office was developed, launching an advertising and marketing campaign. Being lured by expert levels of marketing, new recruits flooded into the region to join this

---

[337] See http://www.counterextremism.com/content/abu-moussa-isis-press-officer-june-2014. See also http://www.theatlantic.com/international/archive/2014/08/isil-press-officer-abu-mosa-killed-by-syrian-army/378994/ accessed 27 January 2024.

new Islamic State. Swift gains of territory in the Anbar area of Iraq and North Syria followed, resulting in the UK proscribing the terrorist group in July 2014.[338] At the peak of its power, the Islamic State became one of the most notorious and influential groups within the Middle East and North Africa, posing a direct terrorist threat not only to those regions but to the nation-states around the world. The sheer level of violence that was directed toward all those who opposed the Islamic State and its ideology was merciless and documented by the film. Such short clips showed the gruesome beheadings of UK, US and Japanese citizens, Syrian opposition forces, and massacres of Sunni Muslim cities such as Tikrit in Iraq.[339]

---

[338] House of Commons Library (2014) The Terrorism Act 2000: Proscribed Organisations, Standard note SN/HA/00815, 25th July 2014, available at researchbriefings.files.parliament.uk/documents/SN00815/SN008 15.pdf, p.8.

[339] N. Khomami (2015) Mohammad Emwazi: who were his victims? The Guardian, 13 November 2015, available at http://www.theguardian.com/uk-news/2015/nov/13/mohammed-emwazi-who-were-his-victims accessed 20 January 2024.

Enter into the frame, Jihadi John. Real name Mohammed Emwazi, he would appear on many short clips, hooded and stood over his latest victim, holding a knife and speaking to the camera. UK security services and the media were shocked to hear a very strong London accent from this hooded figure. Emwazi would then brutally behead the victim on film, which would then be shared through the Islamic State's press office. The actions and ideology of the Islamic State led many inspired individuals to carry out terror attacks in their home nations to show support for the group. In November 2015, an attack took place in Paris, France, and then on a Tunisian holiday resort, resulting in 38 UK citizens' deaths. In Nice, France, on Bastille Day, a lone actor killed 86 civilians and injured 303 by driving a 17-tonne heavy goods vehicle through a crowd of people.[340] The world witnessed beheadings, attacks and other atrocities at large due to the group's efficient use of electronic communications technology.

How terrorist groups use the Internet?

Utilising the Internet to market the Islamic State brand, the group essentially made all its press releases and statements available in over forty languages. Through the Internet, the group could place its message and propaganda directly into the bedrooms and homes of citizens worldwide. Infiltration, unfortunately, influenced people to join the fight in Syria and Iraq or to commit lone Islamist attacks in their home nation-states.[341] It became clear, and remains so, that the Internet and social media outlets have been an absolute gift to terrorist groups.[342]

---

[340] See http://www.bbc.co.uk/news/world-europe-36801671 accessed 20 January 2024.

[341] J. Klausen (2015) Tweeting the Jihad: Social Media Networks of Western Foreign Fighters in Syria and Iraq, *Studies in Conflict & Terrorism* 39(1), 1-22, 3.

[342] *Ibid*. For an example image see https://www.reddit.com/r/jihadpropaganda/ accessed 21 January 2024.

Such outlets, including X, Facebook and YouTube, allow for glorifying such barbarity illustrations and recruiting others to join the cause. Additionally, dedicated websites such as Jihadology publish online Islamist magazines translated into various languages, of course.[343] The Islamic State has created the Dar al-Islam and Dabiq, and Al-Qaeda created Inspire. The Islamic State created a media department and decentralised social media use, illustrating awareness through the Internet. The kidnapping and hostage holding of John Cantlie, who was forced to read out messages from the Islamic State, represents such an example. More readily known as the Cantile Files, the Islamic State essentially shared their messages through him to explain that Western media had misrepresented the group.[344] These video clips, as with all propaganda, were skilfully produced to a high quality. The

---

[343] See http://jihadology.net/category/dar-al-islam-magazine/ and https://azelin.files.wordpress.com/2016/07/al-qacc84_idah-in-the-arabian-peninsula-e2809cinspire-guide-2-nice-operatione2809d.pdf accessed 27 January 2024.

[344] BBC News (2014) Video of British hostage John Cantlie released, 18th September 2014, available at http://www.bbc.co.uk/news/uk-29258201 accessed 20 January 2024.

video clips sent a powerful message. On the one hand, the Islamic State was illustrating their untouchability and power, and on the other, creating fear. For Milton, the mixing of fear and reason makes a potent combination.[345]

The Islamic State's Ministry of Media included the al-Furqan Institute, l'tisaam Media Foundation, Anjad Media Foundations, and the English-based outlet the al-Hayat Media Centre.[346] The al-Furqan manufactured DVDs, and created posters and brochures that the al'tisaam would then disseminate through the Internet in various languages.[347] Through this avenue, they would seek to

---

[345] D. Milton (2014) The Islamic State: An Adaptive Organisation Facing Increasing Challenges, in al-Ubaydi, Lahoud, Milton and Price (editors), The Group That Calls Itself a State: Understanding the Evolution and Challenges of the Islamic State, December 2014, The Combatting Terrorism Centre at West Point, p.53, available at www.ctc.usma.edu accessed 20 January 2024.

[346] *Ibid.*

[347] A. Khan (2014) What ISIL's English-language propaganda tells us about its goals, Aljazeera 20 June 2014, available at http://america.aljazeera.com/watch/shows/america-tonight/articles/2014/6/19/how-isil-is-remakingitsbrandontheinternet.html accessed 20 January 2024. See also H. J. Ingram (2015) The strategic logic of Islamic state information operations, *Australian Journal of International Affairs* 69(6) 729-752, 732.

legitimise their actions and publicise the Caliphate, all aimed at recruitment and gaining the support of course.[348]

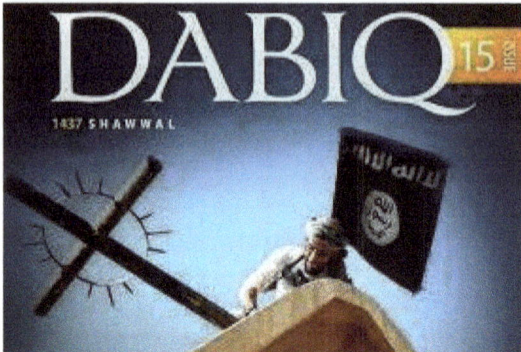

The 15th issue of Dabiq started with:

The spark has been lit here in Iraq, and its heat will continue to intensify – by Allah's permission – until it burns the Crusader armies…[349]

Legitimising the Islamic States struggle against the West and what they referred to as 'the Crusaders', magazines and other media were targeted through the

---

[348] H. J. Ingram (2015) Three Traits of the Islamic State's Information Warfare, *The Rusi Journal* 159(6) 4-11, 5.
[349] Dabiq (2016) Breaking The Cross, Issue 15, 1437 Shawwal, p.1, available at http://jihadology.net accessed 15 January 2024.

interest, beamed into people's homes.[350] Of course, the articles and reports within the magazines were biased and clearly aimed to spread their rather cynical take on Christianity, Judaism and all other forms of religion and non-religion that did not follow their own interpretation of Islam.[351] Full of glossy photos and 'good news stories', terrorist attacks were glamorised and celebrated.[352] One particular story covered the attack in Nice, stating,

Between the release of this issue of Dabiq and the next slaughter to be executed against them [the West] by the hidden soldiers of the Caliphate - who are ordered to attack without delay - the Crusaders can read into why Muslims hate and fight them, why pagan Christians should break their crosses, why liberalist secularists should return to the fitrah (natural human disposition), and why sceptical atheists should recognize their Creator and submit to Him. In essence, we explain why they must

---

[350] *Ibid.*
[351] *Ibid* p.67.
[352] *Ibid* p.10.

abandon their infidelity and accept Islam, the religion of sincerity and submission...[353]

Unfortunately, the expert use of imagery and storytelling resonated with many people, sharing partially their view of an overly liberalised West, explored in an article called, 'Why we hate you and why we fight you.'[354]

How could they use Social Media?

The global population's use of social media is ever-expanding, as documented below. The Islamic State dropped onto this medium, just as many private businesses have to market their brand and how state agencies use it to increase presence, visibility and accountability. At the peak of the Islamic State's power, in 2015, the Director of Europol confirmed the terrorist group was believed to directly control 50,000 different X accounts, the messages from which were then shared by individual Islamists, meaning up to 100,000 X messages per day.[355]

---

[353] *Ibid* p.4.

[354] *Ibid.*

[355] See http://www.dailymail.co.uk/sciencetech/article-3747501/Twitter-s-terror-crackdown-Social-network-says-shut-

The information provided by Europol appears to have been a rather conservative estimate, given that for Berger and Morgan the Islamic State controled over 90,000 X accounts.[356] In August 2016, X (then Twitter) announced they had closed over 235,000 accounts with links to the Islamic State over a six-month period.[357] Examples of such messages read:

You can sit at home and play Call of Duty, or you can come here and respond to the real call of duty...Kill the police and soldiers...carry out lone wolf operations...smash his head with a rock, or slaughter him with a knife, or run him over with your car, or throw him

---

235-000-accounts-linked-Islamic-State-groups-six-months.html accessed 27 January 2024.

[356] J.M. Berger and J. Morgan (2015) The ISIS Twitter Census: Defining and describing the population of ISIS supporters on Twitter, 20 March 2015, Center for Middle East Policy at Brooking, available at http://webcache.googleusercontent.com/search?q=cache:nUpiATbv50wJ:www.brookings.edu/~/media/research/files/papers/2015/03/isis-twitter-census-berger-morgan/isis_twitter_census_berger_morgan.pdf+&cd=1&hl=en&ct=clnk&gl=uk accessed 21 February 2024

[357] See http://www.dailymail.co.uk/sciencetech/article-3747501/Twitter-s-terror-crackdown-Social-network-says-shut-235-000-accounts-linked-Islamic-State-groups-six-months.html accessed 27 October 2016.

down from a high place, or choke him, or poison him…Muslims stand by its black brothers and sisters. Your [You're] all welcome to Islamic State; we will embrace you and love you.[358]

For Ingram, the Islamic State was simply 'more strategic plagiarists than geniuses'.[359] The group simply mirrored the way that private businesses used social media to increase their position.[360] This, unfortunately, resulted in their success.

In order to combat terrorist use of social media, Internet companies started using new software originally designed to remove copyrighted material. Looking for 'hashes' that a unique digital fingerprints assigned to specific videos posted online, the Internet companies were able to automatically target terrorist material. This, in

---

[358] See http://www.memrijttm.org/jihadi-reactions-to-nice-terror-attack-we-want-paris-before-rome.html. See also http://www.independent.co.uk/news/world/middle-east/isis-urges-more-attacks-on-western-disbelievers-9749512.html accessed 27 October 2016.

[359] H. Ingram (2016) Militant Islamist propaganda targeting Muslims in the West: comparing Inspire and Dabiq narratives, Terrorist Use of the Internet: Assessment and Response, Dublin City University, Ireland.

[360] *Ibid.*

turn, led to an increase in the use of the 'darknet', which UK law enforcement agencies continually struggle to police.

Keith Vaz MP, former Chair of the Home Affairs Select Committee, captured the situation well, stating:

Huge corporations like Google, Facebook and Twitter…are consciously failing to tackle this threat and passing the buck by hiding behind their supranational legal status despite knowing that the instigators of terror are using their sites. The companies' failure to tackle this threat has left some parts of the Internet ungoverned and lawless.[361]

Monitoring social media is an extraordinarily difficult task.[362] For Katz with the benefit of encryption, the Islamic State were bypassing the blocking of their X feeds

---

[361] See http://www.independent.co.uk/life-style/gadgets-and-tech/news/facebook-twitter-google-isis-daesh-internet-youtube-social-media-home-affairs-a7208131.html accessed 27 October 2016.

[362] R. Katz (2015) How Islamic State is still Thriving on Twitter, 11 April 2015, InSite Blog on Terrorism & Extremism, available at http://news.siteintelgroup.com/blog/index.php/entry/377-how-the-islamic-state-is-still-thriving-on-twitter accessed 19 November 2016.

by encompassing multiple backup accounts.[363] Perhaps this expert and networked use of social media could be attributed to the average age of the recruit, being 24 years old.[364] For Katz this represented the real threat as they used X to launch recruitment and calls for lone jihad.[365]

The Internet and Application Protocols, Smartphones and Encryption

People born in the early 1990s have not known life without the Internet. Research shows that in 1989, the main types of communication were by letters and landline telephones.[366] From 2014 onwards, less than three in ten 16-24-year-olds continued with this method. Likewise, internet telephony is on the rise, with many providers ditching their old analog systems. Less than 16% of UK households no longer have a landline, and the UK Communications Infrastructure Report suggests this will decrease further, bringing an end to their use.[367] Electronic

---

[363] *Ibid.*

[364] See http://www.popsci.com/terror-on-twitter-how-isis-is-taking-war-to-social-media accessed 27 October 2016.

[365] *Supra* as per Katz.

[366] *Supra* as per D. Anderson (2015) pp.49-50.

[367] *Ibid.*

mailing (emails) and text messaging are likewise going out with the Ark, where the utilisation of smart devices' instant direct messaging applications, more commonly known as chat apps, such as Apple's iMessage and Facebook Messenger, appear to be the current favourite.[368] Coincidingly, the ownership of smartphones and smart devices continues to grow, year on year.[369]

The Internet continues to expand at ever-increasing rate, with around three billion people using Internet calls (VOIP).[370] In addition to these increases in volumes of information sent and received, it was estimated by 2019 that one zettabyte of data travelled over the Internet.[371]

---

[368] D. Anderson (2015) A Question of Trust: Report of the Investigatory Powers Review, London: The Stationary Office, pp.49-50, 'Instant messaging apps have overtaken traditional SMS services. In 2012, 19 billion messages were sent per day on instant messaging apps, compared to 17.6 billion text messages. Since 2012 the number of instant messaging apps has grown considerably.' See also https://www.whatsapp.com, and http://en.people.cn/102774/8568312.html accessed 20 February 2024.

[369] Ibid.

[370] OFCOM, The Communications Market (2016), Telecoms and networks, available at https://www.ofcom.org.uk/__data/assets/pdf_file/0026/26648/uk_telecoms.pdf accessed 20 February 2024.

[371] This is the equivalent of 667 trillion films. See J. Titcomb (2016) World's internet traffic to surpass one zettabyte in

Cisco confirms numbers continue to rise exponentially.[372] The internet is not territorially bound, with servers being placed all over the globe. The servers for many companies, such as Hotmail and Gmail, are based outside the UK.[373] This alone causes issues for law enforcement to trace information sent. Emails, for example, are not confined to the country of origin or receipt; rather, they move freely across borders utilising the quickest path possible. Therefore, although UK legislation may require Internet and service providers to hold data for a certain length of time, the transnational nature means external agreements must be drafted.

The Internet is structured into three categories.[374] The 'surface web' represents webpages that can be found using

---

2016, The Telegraph, 4 February 2016, available at http://www.telegraph.co.uk/technology/2016/02/04/worlds-internet-traffic-to-surpass-one-zettabyte-in-2016/ accessed 20 February 2024.

[372] See https://www.cisco.com/c/en/us/solutions/collateral/executive-perspectives/annual-internet-report/white-paper-c11-741490.html accessed 20 February 2024.

[373] *Supra* as per D. Anderson (2015) p.51.

[374] See https://www.reference.com/technology/basic-structure-internet-91e2893b49bd7bbd accessed 20 November 2016.

standard search engines such as Google.[375] The 'deep web', or 'invisible web', represents parts of the open web that are not indexed by standard search engines.[376] Albeit ominous sounding, this part has many legitimate uses such as, web email, online banking, and videos on demand such as those available through Amazon.[377] It makes up almost 90 percent of Internet usage figures.[378] The 'dark web' or 'darknet' is a small proportion of the invisible web that consists of tens of thousands of websites.[379] To clarify the current acronyms and types of Internet companies:

- Communications Service Providers (CSPs) provide services that transport information electronically. Examples of CSPs include companies such as British Telecom, Skype and TalkTalk, Facebook, and X.

- Companies that simply provide Internet access are referred to as Internet Service Providers (ISPs).

---

[375] *Ibid.*

[376] *Ibid.*

[377] P. Paganini (2012) The good and the bad of the Deep Web, The Hacker New Magazine, 17 September 2012, available at http://securityaffairs.co/wordpress/8719/deep-web/the-good-and-the-bad-of-the-deep-web.html accessed 21 November 2016.

[378] *Ibid.*

[379] *Ibid.*

- Companies that provide applications or services, over the physical networks provided by CSPs and ISPs are called Applications Service Providers (ASPs). Examples of ASPs include Google, Whatsapp, Snapchat, Facebook, Yahoo, Skype and Apple.

Who sent what and when? Who was using the device?

Law enforcement finds it difficult, at times, to attribute internet communication to a specific user of a device. Devices, such as computers, laptops and smartphones, when utilising a network, are assigned an Internet Protocol address (IP). There is only one IP address assigned to an Internet router, which can of course, accommodate many devices. Brown has noted that this infrastructure of the Internet makes it difficult for law enforcement to attribute a particular communication to the potential sender.[380] Family members and visiting

---

[380] C. S. D. Brown (2015) Investigating and Prosecuting Cyber Crime: Forensic Dependencies and Barriers to Justice, International Journal of Cyber Criminology, Vol 9, Issue 1, January-June 2015, p.58, available at http://www.cybercrimejournal.com/Brown2015vol9issue1.pdf accessed 21 November 2016.

friends share the IP address when connecting to the Wi-Fi, and also tend to share smart devices. Another issue is that this IP address does not follow a particular person when traveling and logging on to another Wi-Fi. When using public Wi-Fi, one is advised by providers to use a VPN to protect their devices and accounts from cybercriminals. This in itself creates ghost or proxy IP addresses that are then untraceable.[381] It is therefore, sometimes impossible for the agencies to discover which device was used and by whom.[382]

In an attempt to remedy this problem, the Counter Terrorism and Security Act 2015 (CTSA) was enacted, partially addressing the difficulty arising when IP addresses are shared by a number of users simultaneously, by allowing for the power of internet companies to retain "relevant internet data".[383] However, this attempt appears

---

[381] *Ibid* at p.68.

[382] *Ibid.*

[383] The Home Office Counter-Terrorism and Security Bill Factsheet, Part 3 Internet Protocol (IP) Address Resolution available https://www.gov.uk/government/uploads/system/uploads/attachment_data/file/540538/CTS_Bill_-_Factsheet_5_-_IP_Resolution_v2.pdf accessed 22 November 2016.

to have failed because the CSP can only provide the data of the subscribed person, usually the billpayer. Not therefore the details of the person using a particular device at a particular time.[384] This creates a 'capability gap in communications data' that can have a 'serious impact on the ability of law enforcement to carry out their functions'.[385] Intensifying this gap further is the fact there is now a fragmentation of telecommunications and communications data service providers whose business models are totally reliant on VOIP services. Landline telephone calls are much more traceable, with the provider knowing the endpoints of both parties to the call.[386] Internet and Over-The-Top (OTT) providers are, for the most part, based outside the UK, which makes obtaining data from them more difficult.[387] OTT providers are free at the point of access and require very little subscriber data.[388]

---

[384] *Ibid.*

[385] *Ibid.*

[386] *Supra* as per D. Anderson (2015) p.52.

[387] For OTT see: http://digiday.com/platforms/what-is-over-the-top-ott/.

[388] *Supra* as per D. Anderson (2015) p.52.

Application Protocols and Encryption

The first terrorist group to utilise any type of encryption was Al-Qaeda in the Arabian Peninsula (AQAP). At this stage, it really was in its infancy. The law enforcement investigation into Rajib Karim's communications to Anwar Al-Awlaki illustrated that Karim used a rudimentary multi-layered approach. The process was complex and time-consuming. Karim would write the message into a Microsoft Excel document using macros to encrypt it, then copy and paste that into a Microsoft Word document, saved using the password protection feature. RAR software was then used to compress and encrypt the document and posted online through a shortened URL, rendering it anonymous.[389] In fact, UK law enforcement spent nine months trying to decrypt Karim's computer.[390] Enter into the fray 21st

---

[389] R. Graham (2016) How Terrorists Use Encryption, Combating Terrorism Center, available at https://www.ctc.usma.edu/posts/how-terrorists-use-encryption accessed 21 November 2016.
[390] V. Dodd (2011) British Airways worker Rajib Karim convicted of terrorist plot, Guardian, 28 February 2011, available https://www.theguardian.com/uk/2011/feb/28/british-airways-bomb-guilty-karim accessed 21 November 2016.

Century technology, whereby the 'ubiquity of encryption in commercially available messaging tools and devices has made it increasingly easy for terrorists to communicate securely'.[391]

Encryption has now legitimately developed as a commercial commodity and is readily available. Two main forms exist:

- Encryption in transit: this provides security during the transmission;

- End-to-end encryption: this renders the message unreadable to all but the sender and intended recipient.

The former represents technology used by the banking industry to ensure safe and secure communication. The latter, end-to-end encryption, is when the contents of a message are converted into an unreadable form. Only the person with the correct decryption key can read it, usually, the one receiving it.

---

[391] R. Graham (2016) How Terrorists Use Encryption, Combating Terrorism Center, available at https://www.ctc.usma.edu/posts/how-terrorists-use-encryption accessed 21 November 2016.

Encryption is important for all people in securing privacy, given most use a smart device to store private information, including banking and finance information, photos and contacts, which can then be stored on an iCloud server.[392] It is also important to mention that, particularly since the introduction of applications such as Apple Pay, smartphone and server encryption forms an essential part of providing the customer with a high level of safety.[393]

Ensuring a high level of security forms part of the private companies' obligation to their customers. As such the network provider for the communication exchange is often unable to decrypt a message. Likewise, they are unable to gain entry into an individual's data stored on their smart device.[394] However, with all legitimate technological growth comes criminal exploitation. They

---

[392] See https://support.apple.com/en-gb/HT202303 accessed 20 February 2024.

[393] See https://support.apple.com/en-gb/HT203027 accessed 20 February 2024.

[394] *Ibid.*

almost go hand in hand.[395] Serious organized criminals and, gangs, and terrorists can essentially communicate freely without the watchful eye of the State. It is this particular element that creates a law enforcement capabilities gap. States have been calling for some sort of back door entry key into people's devices and messages for some time now, resulting in a resolute response from companies openly denying the request. Apple for example, confirmed that they have no way to decrypt iMessage and FaceTime data when it is in transit between devices. Apple does not scan the communications and, therefore would not be able to comply with a surveillance order.[396]

Messaging Applications

Commonly known as chat apps, they represented the first of their kind. They used a different type of encryption that stopped at the service providers' servers. This meant

---

[395] R. Smith (1998) Criminal exploitation of new technologies, Australian Institute of Criminology, Trends & Issues in Crime and Criminal Justice No. 93, 1.

[396] *Supra* as per D. Anderson (2015) p.206. See also Apple's website http://www.apple.com/uk/privacy/approach-to-privacy/.

that law enforcement could obtain the electronic communications data records. However, this also allowed cyber criminals access to hack into the service providers' servers and obtain the same data. This led to the idea of using military strength end-to-end encryption, first developed commercially by Telegram. Al-Qaeda operatives started to use this technology immediately.[397] End-to-end encryption protocols are the new norm, if you will, such as Whatsapp, Facebook Messenger, Instagram, Wickr, Line, Signal and Google.[398]

---

[397] See http://gizmodo.com/the-best-and-worst-encrypted-messaging-apps-1782424449 accessed 21 November 2016.

[398] See http://gizmodo.com/the-best-and-worst-encrypted-messaging-apps-1782424449 and http://www.techtimes.com/articles/169154/20160709/9-messaging-apps-with-end-to-end-encryption-facebook-messenger-whatsapp-imessage-and-more.htm accessed 21 November 2016.

Not only is such encryption near impossible to break, without having the user provide assistance, some chat apps can be set up so they delete any messages after an hour or a day. The encryption essentially allows terrorists to communicate freely and law enforcement faces evidential issues because the messages may no longer be available.

According to the Government Communications Headquarters (GCHQ), such devices and applications have become the 'command and control network' of terrorists.[399] In the run-up to and following the terrorist attack in Paris, France, on 15 November 2015, messaging

---

[399] GCHQ chief accuses US tech giants of becoming terrorists, networks of choice, The Guardian, 3 November 2014 available at https://www.theguardian.com/uk-news/2014/nov/03/privacy-gchq-spying-robert-hannigan accessed 21 November 2016.

apps were used, along with disposable 'burner' phones.[400] This allowed them to plan and thereby carry out their attack, resulting in 130 deaths with hundreds more injured.[401] Utilising such technology was advised to would-be terrorists by the Islamic State in their 2016 edition of Dar al-Islam.[402] For Ban Ki-moon, the then Secretary-General of the United Nations, 'the Internet is a prime example of how terrorists can behave in a truly transnational way'.[403] These issues have led to the then Director of Europol to comment:

...as the communications of terrorist networks and criminal groups have moved increasingly [online], it's

---

[400] J. Stone (2016) ISIS Terrorists Used Disposable Burner Phones, Activated Just Hours Before, To Carry Out Paris Attacks, International Business Times, 21 March 2016, available http://www.ibtimes.com/isis-terrorists-used-disposable-burner-phones-activated-just-hours-carry-out-paris-2340265 accessed 21 November 2016.

[401] *Ibid.*

[402] R. Graham (2016) How Terrorists Use Encryption, Combating Terrorism Center, available at https://www.ctc.usma.edu/posts/how-terrorists-use-encryption accessed 19 November 2016.

[403] *Ibid.*

opened up a whole new wave of problems for us even in the open internet, let alone the dark net.[404]

What is the Darknet and how dangerous is it?

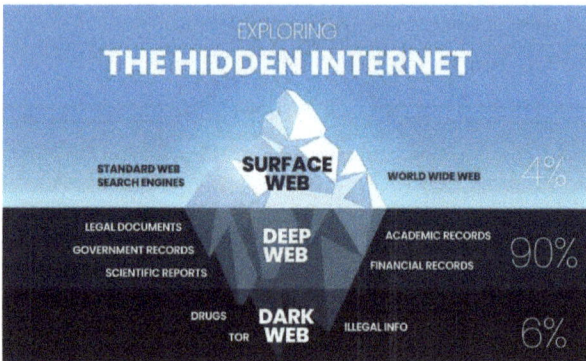

The darknet simply provides a 'World of complete freedom and anonymity, where users say and do what they like, uncensored, unregulated, and outside of society's norms.'[405] The darknet has been around for quite some time already and has represented a rather large thorn in the side of law enforcement. An illegal marketplace exists

---

[404] See http://www.dailymail.co.uk/sciencetech/article-3747501/Twitter-s-terror-crackdown-Social-network-says-shut-235-000-accounts-linked-Islamic-State-groups-six-months.html#ixzz4OIUlFVVU accessed 27 October 2016.
[405] *Ibid.*

where people can buy and sell illegal items such as drugs, counterfeit goods, child pornography and firearms. Europol recognized this in their 2016 TE-SAT report, where they reported that a 'professional, service-based underground economy', has identified the proliferation of cyber-crime and terrorism.[406] The Islamic State is also known to operate through this medium, in raising funds and selling books on how to carry out jihad, how to make bombs and create homemade firearms.[407]

The darknet works by communicating through a network that involves 'onion rooting'.[408] Just like the layers of an onion, this process protects the identity of the people involved in the communication by wrapping layers around it. According to Lakhani, this renders the communication impenetrable and untraceable.[409] Jihadi forums and chat rooms play out under the cloak of

---

[406] Europol (2016) EU Terrorism Situation and Trend report TE-SAT 2016, Hague: Europol, pp.8-9.

[407] http://uk.businessinsider.com/isis-is-using-the-dark-web-2015-7 accessed 21 November 2016.

[408] http://uk.businessinsider.com/isis-is-using-the-dark-web-2015-7. See also http://www.pri.org/stories/2016-05-13/how-isis-recruits-online-using-encryption-chat-rooms-and-even-dating-sites accessed 21 November 2016.

[409] *Ibid.*

anonymity, allowing terrorists and supporters to communicate without fear of detection.[410] These networks allow for the transfer of unique funds which are undetectable, making available for purchase explosives, firearms (of a type that is illegal in the UK), and fraudulent passports along with other items.[411]

The Tor software programme is one of the only ways to gain access to the darknet.[412] Tor has been in operation since October 2003 and is used legitimately by many people who simply do not want to be tracked online. It is designed to stop third-party trackers and advertisements

---

[410] *Ibid.*

[411] See: http://www.huffingtonpost.com/kevin-goodman/internet-black-markets_b_4111000.html. See: http://www.foxnews.com/tech/2015/04/23/darknet-danger-organs-murder-credit-card-info-all-for-sale-on-internet.html accessed 20 November 2016. See also the Dark Wallet, taken from N. Bertrand (2015) ISIS is taking full advantage of the darkest corners of the Internet, Business Insider UK, http://uk.businessinsider.com/isis-is-using-the-dark-web-2015-7?r=US&IR=T accessed 20 February 2024. And semtex explosive, taken from J. Patrice (2016) Bombs used by ISIS in Brussels terror attacks are for sale online, NewsGrio, http://www.newsgrio.com/articles/world/uk/244032-bombs-used-by-isis-in-brussels-terror-attacks-are-for-sale-online.html accessed 20 February 2024.

[412] See https://www.google.co.uk/#q=Tor accessed 20 February 2024.

from following the users' keystrokes. Cookies are cleared automatically, along with browsing history.[413] Whilst it does allow for a person to access the deeper realms of the darknet, called 'Onionland', many use this non-profit project simply to ensure online privacy.[414] Again, as with all legitimate technological growth comes criminal exploitation. Within the free spaces, 'Onionland' allows criminals to work, offer services and effectively 'cloak themselves in obscurity with specialised software that guarantees encryption and anonymity between users, as well as protocols or domains that the average person will never stumble across.'[415]

Although in operation since 2003, and despite concerns that terrorists could be able to launch more advanced attacks and remain anonymous, there is no evidence it has been using for this purpose. Europol's TE-

---

[413] See https://www.torproject.org accessed 20 February 2024.

[414] See http://www.pcworld.com/article/2046227/meet-darknet-the-hidden-anonymous-underbelly-of-the-searchable-web.html accessed 20 February 2024.

[415] http://www.pcworld.com/article/2046227/meet-darknet-the-hidden-anonymous-underbelly-of-the-searchable-web.html accessed 20 February 2024.

SAT reports confirmed that the Islamic State did hold an advanced level of encryption know-how.[416] Policing the Internet represents a huge challenge to law enforcement, particularly the dark online spaces. Brown confirms that law enforcement agencies face a significant capabilities gap in expertise and budget.[417] UK Government committed an extra £1.9 billion to be invested in dealing with cybercrime in November 2015.[418] £650 million was invested in a new National Cyber Security Programme and in October 2016, the Centre was launched.[419] Since then, in 2023, investment means new innovation can continue.[420] This investment will increase the expertise

---

[416] *Supra* as per Europol (2016).

[417] C. S. D. Brown (2015) Investigating and Prosecuting Cyber Crime: Forensic Dependencies and Barriers to Justice, International Journal of Cyber Criminology, Vol 9, Issue 1, January-June 2015, p.92, available at http://www.cybercrimejournal.com/Brown2015vol9issue1.pdf accessed 20 February 2024.

[418] https://www.gov.uk/government/speeches/chancellors-speech-to-gchq-on-cyber-security accessed 20 February 2024

[419] See https://www.ncsc.gov.uk/section/about-ncsc/what-we-do accessed 20 February 2024.

[420] See https://portal.lancaster.ac.uk/portal/news/article/lancaster-university-to-lead-major-12-million-project-to-unlock-cyber-security-potential-across-north-west-1 accessed 20 February 2024.

lacking, with GCHQ reportedly planning to share their cryptography and intelligence analysis knowledge.[421] In addition GCHQ and the NCA have co-located a Joint Operations Cell (JOC) in order to increase their abilities.[422]

Clearly, the Islamic State's digital communicational strategy proved first class. Propaganda led to the radicalisation of thousands of citizens across the EU, resulting in terrorist attacks being committed or thwarted.[423] To capture the potential damage, we can look to the example in 2015, where a 15-year-old boy from Blackburn, England, plotted with an Australian counterpart to behead Australian police officers at the ANZAC day celebrations. This case still represents the youngest of those convicted of terrorism-related

---

[421] R. Perez (2016) GCHQ to fund startups to fight cyber-crime, SC Magazine available at http://www.scmagazineuk.com/gchq-to-fund-startups-to-fight-cyber-crime/article/524540/ accessed 20 February 2024.

[422] http://www.nationalcrimeagency.gov.uk/news/736-gchq-and-nca-join-forces-to-ensure-no-hiding-place-online-for-criminals accessed 20 February 2024.

[423] S. Coates (2015) PM: seven terror attacks in UK stopped in last year, The Times, 16 November 2015, available at http://www.thetimes.co.uk/tto/news/uk/article4615198.ece accessed 20 November 2016.

offences.[424] Despite being all but depleted, the ideology of the Islamic State and others, still resonates and reverberates through cities and towns. Concern has recently been raised due to the current conflict regarding Israel and the Gaza strip. UK law enforcement has warned of an increase in the potential of an attack.[425] Clearly concerned with a potential rise in radicalisation, radical activity has been sparked by the conflict, with the main threat identified as coming from 'low sophistication, lone actors'.[426] Often referred to as 'clean skins', such low-sophistication attacks include those committed in London in 2017, where perpetrators use rented vehicles and knives rather than an organised and planned event using explosives.[427] The current threat of course, cannot be

---

[424] BBC News (2015) Anzac Day terror plot: Blackburn teenager admits inciting attack, 23 July 2015, available at retrieved from http://www.bbc.co.uk/news/uk-england-manchester-33633915 accessed 20 February 2024.

[425] J. Dunne, 'Police warn of rising threat of terror attack in UK due to radicalisation sparked by Israel-Gaza conflict', The Standard, 22 January 2024, at https://www.standard.co.uk/news/crime/terror-attack-risk-uk-radicalisation-israel-gaza-conflict-b1133526.html (last visited 28 January 2024).

[426] *Ibid.*

[427] For example see London Bridge attack: What happened - BBC News (last visited 28 January 2024).

underestimated by the UK's security services, given the controversy surrounding the conflict and the judgement of the International Court of Justice on 26 January 2024 imposing six provisional measures to be implemented. Following the terrorist attack on Israel by Hamas, approximately tens of thousands of Palestinians have been killed, and according to Amnesty International, millions of people have been displaced, deprived of adequate food, water, shelter, sanitation and medical assistance.[428] Causing internal security concerns across the world, in the UK, Jewish and Muslim citizens and communities have been warned of the likelihood of hate crimes.[429] It remains to be seen if this conflict results in an increase of Prevent referrals.

---

[428] See Israel must comply with key ICJ ruling ordering it do all in its power to prevent genocide against Palestinians in Gaza - Amnesty International (last visited 28 January 2024).

[429] K. Nicholson, '4 Ways The Israel Conflict Has Impacted UK Life Over The Last Week', Huffington Post, 13 October 2023, at https://www.huffingtonpost.co.uk/entry/how-israel-conflict-impact-life-europe_uk_6529167ae4b03ea0c004b0c0 (last visited 28 January 2024).

The law and policy to prevent a terror attack, how far can the state go?

Since 2000, the UK has enacted 11 counter-terrorism laws, not including those dealing with powers of surveillance afforded to law enforcement. In addition to the legal measures, the UK government's counter-terrorism policy can be found under the CONTEST document, newly published in 2023. It outlines that since 2018, there have been nine terrorist attacks. Since March 2017, 39 potential attacks have been disrupted.[430]

---

[430] HM Government (2023) CONTEST, July 2023, CP903 available at https://assets.publishing.service.gov.uk/media/650b1b8d52e73c000d54dc82/CONTEST_2023_English_updated.pdf accessed 20 February 2024.

The overarching aim of this policy is to reduce the risk terrorism poses. CONTEST is split into four parts,

- Prevent: to prevent people from being radicalised and drawn to supporting and/or committing an act of terrorism.

- Pursue: to actively investigate and pursue terrorists to disrupt planned attacks.

- Protect: to protect citizens and the UK State by reducing any vulnerabilities.

- Prepare: to mitigate and lessen the impact of any successful terrorist attack.

Remaining within the ambit of Prevent, the idea essentially is to secure early intervention to support people that are vulnerable and susceptible to radicalisation. In essence, anyone can make a Prevent referral; however, many institutions, including schools, colleges and universities, local authorities and health, must consider this safeguarding duty on a daily basis. Those referred to Prevent are then assessed and a Channel Panel meets to assess the risk and put in place support for the individual.

This is a voluntary process which means individuals referred must consent. There have been some challenges to this end. Some have been referred and consented but have then continued to commit a terrorist attack. Some who should have been referred but were not have gone to commit and act. The same can be said for those convicted of terrorism-related offences who claim to have been rehabilitated, who likewise go on to commit terrorism. Examples include:

- Salman Abedi, on 22 May 2017, detonated a homemade explosive in the entrance to the Manchester Arena at the end of an Ariana Grande concert, killing himself in the process along with 22 others with 1017 suffering injury. During the Manchester Arena Inquiry, which concluded in 2023, it was learned that there were missed opportunities to refer Abedi to Prevent. Abedi had travelled to participate in the Libyan Civil War, meeting members of Al-Qaeda in the Islamic Maghreb.

- During law enforcement anti-terror Operation Guava in 2010, Usman Khan and eight other men were charged with planning a terrorist attack. Their plan included bombing the London Stock Exchange, the UK Houses of Parliament, and the US Embassy, and targeting two rabbis at two synagogues, the Dean of St Paul Cathedral and the home of the then Major of London Boris Johnson. In 2012 Khan pleaded guilty and received an indeterminate prison sentence with a minimum of eight years. The indeterminate element was appealed by Khan in which his sentence was instead changed to 16 years, meaning he could automatically be released after serving eight years. In December 2018, he was released under a supervision order, after completing the de-radicalisation programmes, including the Desistance and Disengagement Programme. Considered at the time as a success story for a Cambridge University rehabilitation programme. Khan attended Cambridge University's Learning Together 'Five Year Celebration' in 2019 in London, despite his temporary release licence not permitting him to travel to London. He went on to kill two of the organisers, injure three other people, with his life coming to an abrupt end on

London Bridge, where armed police shot him as he flashed his fake suicide vest.

The legacy of Usman Khan is the passing of a new law, the Counter-Terrorism and Sentencing Act 2021, which extends the minimum prison terms for serious terrorism-related offences to 14 years, and stops the automatic release system. This Act also introduces for the first time, polygraph licence testing conditions for those convicted of terrorism offences.

The Terrorist Threat and Impact on Freedoms

The Prevent duty was placed on the statute book by way of the Counter Terrorism and Security Act 2015. With all counter-terrorism laws relying on the legal definition of terrorism under the Terrorism Act 2000 (TA 2000), terrorism remains defined in broad terms. In continuing the theme regarding these pre-emptive and rather critically termed 'pre-crime' measures, the Terrorism Act 2006 has since been bolstered by the Counter-Terrorism and Border Security Act 2019, which criminalises the *expression of opinion or belief* in a proscribed organisation. More and more emphasis is being placed on online spaces, where such views can be shared more freely and with greater ease. There have been several cases where the Terrorism Act 2006 has been employed, which critics argue limits the freedom of expression in the UK. Such cases include:

- *R v Mohammed Gul* who was arrested in 2014 for posting a message on Facebook that was deemed to be supportive of the Islamic State. Gul was charged and found guilty of the glorification of terrorism and was sentenced to four years in prison.[431]

- R v Azhar Ahmed, who was arrested in 2012 for posting a message on Facebook that was deemed to be offensive to soldiers who had died in Afghanistan. Ahmed was charged under section 127 of the Communications Act 2003 and section 1 of the Terrorism Act 2006. Despite removing the posts and sending messages of apology, he was found guilty and

---

[431] *R v Gul* [2013] UKSC 64. *Gul* was charged under s1 Terrorism Act 2006.

given a 2-year Community Order, fined £300 and
sentenced to 240 hours of community service.[432]

- Mohammed Shabir Ali who was arrested in 2016 for
  publishing a video on YouTube that was deemed to
  be supportive of the Islamic State. He was also found
  to have been raising funds for the terrorist group al-
  Shabaab and sentenced to three years in prison.[433]

It could of course be argued that the Counter-
Terrorism and Border Security Act 2019 is too broad and
can be used to target individuals who have not actually
engaged in acts of terrorism, rather, however grotesque,
have merely expressed support. Legal measures such as
these, although designed to provide security and safety,
can have a negative effect on freedom of expression.
Concerns have been raised, particularly by those from

---

[432] R v Ahmed [2012] District Judge Goodwin presiding, Huddersfield Magistrates Court, at https://www.judiciary.uk/wp-content/uploads/JCO/Documents/Judgments/azhar-ahmed-sentencing-remarks-09102012.pdf (last visited 12 April 2023).

[433] S. Robson, 'Islamic extremist jailed for helping fund jihadis in Africa now working as Sainsbury's home delivery driver', The Mirror, 9 October 2016 at https://www.mirror.co.uk/news/uk-news/ali-twins-jailed-mohammed-shafiq-9013745 (last visited 12 April 2023).

minority communities, who may already feel marginalised and vulnerable to state scrutiny. One study conducted by the human rights group Liberty found that individuals and organisations were more hesitant to express opinions on contentious political issues for fear of being accused of glorifying terrorism.[434] This would fit with Woods's argumentation surrounding the enforcement and subsequent impact of the Terrorism Act 2006.[435] Another study by Article 19, International Centre Against Censorship, found that the glorification of terrorism offence had a disproportionate impact on minority communities, particularly Muslims.[436] The study found that the offence was often applied in a way that targeted speech that was critical of governmental policies or supportive of the Palestinian cause, rather than speech that genuinely supported terrorism. For Choudhury and

---

[434] See https://www.libertyhumanrights.org.uk/right/freedom-of-expression/ for further information (last visited 12 April 2023).

[435] L. Woods, 'Freedom of Expression in the European Union'. European Public Law, 2006, 12. pp. 371-401.

[436] S. Coliver, 'Striking a Balance: Hate Speech, Freedom of Expression and Non-discrimination, University of Essex, 1992, at https://www.article19.org/data/files/pdfs/publications/striking-a-balance.pdf (last visited 12 April 2023).

Fenwick, this fits within the broader issues and concerns raised that 'counter-terrorism laws and policies are increasingly alienating Muslims, especially young people and students, and that counter-terrorism measures may themselves feed and sustain terrorism'.[437]

International human rights organizations, including the United Nations have also criticised the impact of the Terrorism Act 2006 on the freedom of expression. In a report on counter-terrorism measures and human rights, the UN Special Rapporteur on promoting and protecting human rights and fundamental freedoms while countering terrorism expressed concern about the impact of glorifying terrorism offence on the freedom of expression in the UK.[438] This has had little to no effect on the UK government's counter-terrorism laws or strategy, and in

---

[437] T. Choudhury & H. Fenwick, 'The impact of counter-terrorism measures on Muslim communities', International Review of Law, Computers & Technology, 2011, 25:3.

[438] United Nations, United Nations Human Rights Office of the High Commissioner, A/77/345: Promotion and protection of human rights and fundamental freedoms while countering terrorism - Note by the Secretary-General, 16 September 2022 at https://www.ohchr.org/en/documents/thematic-reports/a77345-promotion-and-protection-human-rights-and-fundamental-freedoms (last visited 12 April 2023).

terms of policing and the enforcement of the terrorism-related offences, powers have been extended to deter them taking place online. In 2016, the UK enacted the Investigatory Powers Act (IPA), which essentially seeks to digitise law enforcement powers of surveillance.

The Investigatory Powers Act 2016 and Ecomms

Investigatory Powers Act 2016

The Investigatory Powers Act 2016 overhaled the UKs surveillance framework, allowing for the collection and retention of the contents of online communications. Forming a significant part of the UK's legal surveillance framework, it provides a 21st Century type of support to already existing powers under Regulation of Investigatory Powers Act 2000 (RIPA), the Intelligence Services Act

1994 (ISA) and the Security Services Act 1985 (SSA).[439] The IPA focuses more on electronic communications data surveillance and bulk powers, with the aim set to combat terrorist communication and criminality more generally online.[440] The IPA is, entirely focused on powers related to the surveillance of electronic communications data (ecomms), leaving other powers, such as CHIS management under RIPA. The Rt. Hon. Dominic Grieve KC noted this in the Intelligence and Security Committee's report into the IPA.[441] Grieve's Report found that although the IPA makes some attempt to improve transparency, the Intelligence and Security Committee were disappointed to note that it does not cover all the agencies' intrusive capabilities.[442]

Part One of IPA introduced wider safeguards in protecting personal data and privacy rights. This includes

---

[439] Investigatory Powers Act 2016, s 251.

[440] Investigatory Powers Act 2016, s259.

[441] The Rt. Hon. Dominic Grieve QC MP (2016) Intelligence and Security Committee of Parliament, Report on the draft Investigatory Powers Bill, 9 February, HC 795, p.1.

[442] The Rt. Hon. Dominic Grieve QC MP (2016) Intelligence and Security Committee of Parliament, Report on the draft Investigatory Powers Bill, 9 February, HC 795, p.1.

the criminal offence for the misuse of ecomms powers.[443]
Part Two of IPA introduced the use of targeted
interception and needs to be read alongside Part Five,
which introduces targeted equipment interference. Parts
Three and Four deal with obtaining, collecting, retaining,
and accessing E-comms data. Parts Six and Seven brought
about wider powers of ecomms surveillance, with bulk
powers that can be used more broadly and less targeted,
and the retention and use of personal datasets. Part Eight
provides new independent judicial oversight, the so-called
double lock system, and Part Nine providing the Secretary of
State review the operation of the IPA and to report to
Parliament.[444] The Home Office published this report and
laid it before Parliament on 9 February 2023.[445] The report
concluded that the IPA achieved its goals broadly, but

---

[443] Investigatory Powers Act 2016, s 11. Ecomms is the
phrase used to describe Electronic Communications.

[444] Investigatory Powers Act 2016, s260. See also House
of Lords Second Reading 27 June 2016, Volume 773, Column
1361-1362, available at https://hansard.parliament.uk/lords/2016-
06-27/debates/1606278000466/InvestigatoryPowersBill. See also
Investigatory Powers Act 2016, s 19 and 23.

[445] See
https://www.gov.uk/government/publications/report-on-the-
operation-of-the-investigatory-powers-act-2016 Accessed 20
February 2024.

recognised that substantial reform may be needed in light of technological advancements. The led to an independent review by Lord Anderson, published in June 2023.[446] His Lordship review related to Bulk Personal Datasets, Internet Connection Records, Data Retention Notices and Targeted Examination Warrants. We will return to this report towards the end of this Chapter.

While IPA includes a human rights focus and the double lock authorisation process, it remains primarily concerned with national security and public safety. As such it contains provisions that have implications for the freedom of expression.

One of the provisions that relates to the freedom of expression is the power to intercept and retain communications data.[447] This includes the content of communications, as defined in the case of *R v Coulson*, as well as metadata such as the time and location of

---

[446] See https://assets.publishing.service.gov.uk/government/uploads/system/uploads/attachment_data/file/1166726/Independent_Review_of_the_Investigatory_Powers_Act_2016-FINAL.pdf accessed 20 February 2024.

[447] Investigatory Powers Act 2016, Part Two.

communications.[448] Another provision of IPA that relates to freedom of expression is the power to require internet service providers to retain communications data for up to 12 months.[449] Law enforcement agencies can access this data without a warrant in certain circumstances.[450] The IPA also includes provisions for the bulk collection of personal data, which allows intelligence agencies to collect and retain large amounts of data on individuals without individualised suspicion.[451] This is set to change as the IPA is up for review.

The bulk powers of surveillance are the most important and controversial parts of IPA, aimed at closing the UK's law enforcement agencies' technological capabilities gaps. They are concerned with finding new investigative leads and locating potential persons of interest who might pose a threat, perhaps more accurately

---

[448] Investigatory Powers Act 2016, s136, and *R v Coulson* [2013] EWCA Crim 1026.

[449] Investigatory Powers Act 2016, s62. See also House of Commons Second Reading, 15 March 2016, Column 830, at http://www.publications.parliament.uk/pa/cm201516/cmhansrd/cm160315/debtext/160315-0001.htm#16031546000001 (last visited 13 April 2023).

[450] Investigatory Powers Act 2016, s158.

[451] Investigatory Powers Act 2016, s199.

described as finding the needles in haystacks.[452] The former Director General of the UK's Security Service (MI5), Lord Evans in his evidence presented to the First Sitting Committee Debate on the IPA in March 2016, made such representations.[453] In his example, he suggested that using bulk powers allows law enforcement to find people who *might* be members of IS and thereby *may* pose a threat by:

…look[ing] at *all individuals* from the UK who are known to have travelled into or out of the Middle East and the area around Syria over the past six months.[454]

Then narrow the field of search by looking for ecomms data on individuals who have been in a certain area:

---

[452] S. Hale-Ross, 'Digital Privacy, Terrorism and Law Enforcement: The UK's Response to Terrorist Communication', (2019 Routledge) p63.

[453] First sitting Committee Debate Session 2015-16, Investigatory Powers Bill, Publications on the Internet, Column 23, 24 March 2016 at http://www.publications.parliament.uk/pa/cm201516/cmpublic/in vestigatorypowers/160324/am/160324s01.htm (last visited 13 April 2023).

[454] *Ibid.*

...Put[ing] all those elements of data together and you will end up with perhaps a few dozen...You might then say, "Let's take all those phones and see which of those telephones has been in first or second-order contact with known extremists"...That might refine it down from 150 to half a dozen. Then you might start to think, "Actually, there's quite a high likelihood, although one cannot be certain, that these half a dozen might be people of security interest"...At that point, having gone through those various layers of putting different sorts of data together, comparing, contrasting and seeing what comes out, you might say, "Perhaps for those half a dozen, some more targeted form of surveillance is justified"...Once you have done that, [subject to authorisations] you might then find that some of them are self-evidently not, because they are BBC journalists who have been following the story or similar...But you might find that you have one or two who look as though they might be IS activists...so you put some resource into establishing what they are doing and who they are associating with.[455]

---

[455] *Ibid.*

According to Evans, this typical data processing has been used for some time and has proved crucial in identifying those involved in terrorist planning.[456]

Evans position was challenged during the IPA's passage through Parliament, with arguments surrounding the necessity and proportionate nature of the initial collection and retention of bulk data.[457] The bulk powers are extraordinarily broad in scope and capture.[458] Eric King, the Director of 'Don't Spy On Us' raised additional concerns regarding the Government Communications Headquarters (GCHQ) interception practices, which disproportionately allows for the collection of up to 50 billion pieces of communication daily.[459] For King, this initial collection stage employs the latest artificial intelligence and algorithmic software, which lacks safeguards and accountability.[460] Optic Nerve, a computer programme used by GCHQ that intercepted up to 50 million pieces of webcam traffic reinforces Kings point.

---

[456] *Ibid.*
[457] *Ibid.*
[458] *Ibid* at Column 7.
[459] *Ibid* at Column 13.
[460] *Ibid.*

With current 21st Century facial recognition software, this means that surveillance powers could be used without the need for further warrants.[461] Accountability is again problematic as an algorithm will complete the process with little or no human contact.[462]

This aspect of ecomms powers presents more controversy surrounding the collection, retention and access to the different types of data. RIPA divides communications data into three categories:

1) **Traffic Data** that identifies the person or suspect, the apparatus used, and the location or address of where a communication is transmitted including the information about a computer file or a program, which has been accessed or run in the course of sending or receiving a communication.[463] Traffic data includes location software used by mobile telephones (geodata) when either stationary or moving, and private Wi-Fi networks. According to the Acquisition

---

[461] *Ibid.*

[462] *Ibid* at Column 14.

[463] Regulation of Investigatory Powers Act 2000, s 21(4)(a), 21(6).

Code, website addresses beyond the Uniform Resource Locator (url) first slash are not traffic data but classed as contents. IP addresses remain classed as traffic data;[464]

2) **Service Use Information** relates to the use of a specific telecommunications service. The service provider records and holds the usage frequency and specific details of the service used by the citizen, such as the amount of data downloaded;[465]

3) **Subscriber information** includes data such as their postal address, telephone numbers and email address. It can also cover their bank account data and personal

---

[464] Acquisition Code, paragraph 2.20 states, '...traffic data may identify a server or domain name (i.e. a web site) but not a web page'. As pointed out by the Interception of Communications Commissioners Office, there is a degree of ambiguity arising out of the absence of any definition of 'content' within RIPA. See the Interception of Communications Commissioner's submission to D. Anderson Q.C. (2015). Also note the Acquisition Code provides at 2.26 and at 42 that IP addresses can be stored by a service provider in conjunction with subscriber information, in which case it would need to be treated as subscriber information, not traffic data.

[465] Regulation of Investigatory Powers Act 2000, s 21(4)(b) and s 22(4).

information divulged at the time the citizen requested an account with the service provider.[466]

Whilst all types are retained, access to the collected E-comms data is highly restricted. Public authorities for example can only request service use information and subscriber information, whereas law enforcement can access all three types.[467] Critics argue that the indiscriminate collection of E-comms could have an adverse effect on free expression, as people may be less likely to express their opinions or engage in political activities if they feel their privacy is being violated. Undoubtedly, these powers represent a significant invasion of privacy and could potentially be used to target whistle-blowers and investigative journalists. The powers provided here criminalise the unauthorised disclosure of data, which could of course be used to prosecute whistle-blowers and journalists who publish classified information.

---

[466] Regulation of Investigatory Powers Act 2000, s 21(4)(c).

[467] Regulation of Investigatory Powers Act 2000, ss 4, 6. See also Investigatory Powers Act 2016, ss 10, 15, 18, 20, 40, 56, and Schedule 9, 1.

Section 176 of IPA introduces the legalised hacking power, more professionally termed 'bulk equipment interference.' This is increasingly by law enforcement to mitigate the inability to acquire intelligence through conventional bulk interception, and to access data directly from computers and other smart devices. Following the *R v Coulson* case authority, law enforcement can legally hack into Internet servers, such as cloud storage systems and email accounts, and view the content without the person affected knowing.[468] For Martin, this is a step too far in that he argues the UK's GCHQ lack clear lawful authority to conduct such operations.[469] In either case, this is perhaps one of the most intrusive powers available to law enforcement, which has the potential to effectively place a camera into people's homes and hands, simply by hacking into their personal computers and smart devises. The intrusiveness grows naturally, as the 21st Century citizen is, varying according to age and degree of course,

---

[468] *R v Coulson* [2013] EWCA Crim 1026.

[469] A. J. Martin (2105) GCHQ v Privacy International: Computer hacking tribunal showdown begins, The Register, 1 December 2015, at http://www.theregister.co.uk/2015/12/01/gchq_privacy_internatio nal_investigatory_powers_tribunal/ (last visited 13 April 2023.

surgically attached to their technology that tends to ever more increasingly hold sensitive and personal data. In order to facilitate access to smart devices, the IPA has introduced two new powers, the National Security notice and the technical capabilities notice. Both these elements target applications providers and encryption.

For law enforcement, these two powers facilitate access to communications data or other information saved on devices, that would otherwise not be available to them. Ecomms plays a pivotal role in gaining valuable information, allowing them to build an accurate picture of the suspect and can sometimes represent the only method available by which law enforcement can acquire the data.'[470] The Rt. Hon. Sir Malcolm Rifkind's research findings into the murder of Fusilier Lee Rigby on the 22nd May 2013, found that such bulk powers allow the security services to see what the suspect has been looking at and downloading from the Internet.[471] One of the terrorists,

---

[470] *Ibid.*

[471] The Rt. Hon. Sir Malcolm Rifkind MP (2013), Intelligence and Security Committee, Access to communications data by the intelligence and security Agencies, February 2024, Cm8514, p.59.

Adebowale came to the attention of law enforcement due to his online activities, and accessing of extremist material.[472] Although parts of Rifkind's report is redacted in the interests of national security, it shows Adebowale had been looking at the *Inspire* magazine, created by al-Qaeda in the Arabian Peninsula (AQAP) to disseminate extremist information on the Internet in English.[473]

This is where argumentation surrounding the competing interests of Ecomms surveillance and the freedom of expression collide. It is also where we see arguments form around protecting and securing the needs of the many (collective security), against the needs of the few (individual freedoms and rights).

The End of Encryption: National security and technical capabilities notices

Towards the end of the IPA is one of the most intrusive powers to ever be placed on the statue book. The *national security notice* places an operator under an obligation to carry out any conduct, including the provision of

---

[472] *Ibid* at p.59.
[473] *Ibid* at p.59-60.

services or amenities, in order to facilitate an investigation by law enforcement.[474] Like bulk powers, the Secretary of State must first make the order based on proportionality, which must then be approved by an independent Judicial Commissioner.[475] A life-span of the measure is applied to the notice at the discretion of the Secretary of State, however judicial authority will be required that may offer further safeguards.[476]Section 252 of IPA, provides that the Secretary of State can give any relevant service operator a *technical capability notice* imposing an obligation onto the operator to remove any electronic protection applied.[477] Otherwise known as encryption, this power places the operator under the obligation to decrypt the communication or smart device, permitting law enforcement agencies unrestricted access per the notice's conditions. This power can be imposed extra-jurisdictionally, which places many operators in a difficult position in terms of privacy protection requirements.[478] It

---

[474] Investigatory Powers Act 2016, s 252(3).
[475] Investigatory Powers Act 2016, s 252(1).
[476] Investigatory Powers Act 2016, s 252(7).
[477] Investigatory Powers Act 2016, s 253(5)(c), and s 254.
[478] Investigatory Powers Act 2016, s 253(8).

also has the potential to weaken the security model of many device and applications providers.

Encryption is as ubiquitous as computing itself and many people, including private and public companies, rely on it for cyber security. Apple in particular noted their concern that removing encryption will put law-abiding citizens' at risk from cyber criminals, rather than actually affect the cyber criminals who can continue to access other means of encryption.[479] Apple states that, 'surely such an intrusive power, if allowed at all, should only be targeted at the most serious of criminal suspects', rather than on mass that overwhelmingly and inevitably includes innocent people.[480] Apple's formal submission to the UK Joint Committee said:

We believe it would be wrong to weaken security for hundreds of millions of law-abiding customers so that it will also be weaker for the very few who pose a threat. In

---

[479] Apple Inc. and Apple Distribution International— written evidence (IPB0093) submitted to the Joint Committee on the Draft Investigatory Powers Bill, available at https://www.parliament.uk/documents/joint-committees/draft-investigatory-powers-bill/written-evidence-draft-investigatory-powers-committee.pdf (last visited 13 April 2023).

[480] *Ibid.*

this rapidly evolving cyber-threat environment, companies should remain free to implement strong encryption to protect customers.[481]

Many Internet service providers are located overseas, meaning they could be placed in the impossible position of choosing which law, which authority to follow, and which to disregard. Apple for example has offices registered in Ireland, meaning they are subject to European Union data protection laws, and the USA where US law controls access to that data by law enforcement.[482] In the US for example any failure to follow requirements under Title III of the US Omnibus Crime Control and Safe Streets Act, would subject Apple to criminal

---

[481] Joint Committee on the Draft Investigatory Powers Bill (2016) Report of Session 2015-2016, 11 February, HL Paper 93 and HC 651 available at http://www.publications.parliament.uk/pa/jt201516/jtselect/jtinvpowers/93/9302.htm. See also http://www.computerworlduk.com/security/draft-investigatory-powers-bill-what-you-need-know-3629116/

[482] See *R (on the application of David Davis MP, Tom Watson MP, Peter Brice and Geoffrey Lewis v The Secretary of State for the Home Department* [2015] EWHC 2092, [6]-[8], [11].

sanctions for any unauthorised interception of content in transit.[483]

The Investigatory Powers Act 2016 Review

Following the Home Office report and Lord Andersons independent report, King Charles III in his speech officially opening Parliament in 2023, announced the Investigatory Powers (Amendment) Bill, to deliver urgent changes to protect the British people. It is somewhat clear that since 2016, the threat posed to the UK has developed significantly. Of course, this goes hand in hand with extremely fast moving machine learning, machine to machine communication and AI. Such technological advancements have been linked to the Bulk Personal Datasets that are stored by law enforcement. The new Law Enforcement Data Service (LEDS) came into action in March 2022, with more features due to come in 2025, at which point it will replace the Police National

---

[483] Apple Inc. and Apple Distribution International—written evidence (IPB0093) submitted to the Joint Committee on the Draft Investigatory Powers Bill, available at https://www.parliament.uk/documents/joint-committees/draft-investigatory-powers-bill/written-evidence-draft-investigatory-powers-committee.pdf accessed 24 January 2024.

Computer and Police National Database. LEDS will revolutionise how personal datasets are stored and accessed, creating a new centralised database, like something out of a James Bond movie. Machine learning will assist in the uploading, storage and access to facial images and speech samples. In his Lordships review, he recommends that part 7 of the IPA should introduce a new type personal dataset that sets out a low to none expectation of privacy. According to the Government, this would only apply to those datasets that are already publicly available. The new Bill would also create an additional condition, which permits authorities to access internet connection records to identify individuals accessing specific internet sites and services, where and when necessary to address serious crime or protect national security.

Despite the proliferation of laws and measures aimed at countering the terrorism threat and the introduction of greater powers of Ecomms data surveillance, there remains the backdrop of the use of the Internet by terrorists and extremists, to radicalise and recruit others to join their cause. Since the IPA, social media continues to grow, with new internet companies setting up shop and then disappearing after 12 months, along with the criminal exploitation of the online spaces. Paralleled with the UK Governments historic adoption of *suspect policing*, social media now represents the last remaining piece of puzzle, facing new specialist legislation and regulation. To facilitate the removal of terrorist and extremist content that serve to radicalise others, the UK, along with other nation-states have and are attempting to regulate the Internet, and social media.

More Specialist Legislation: Social Media Regulation and Freedom of Expression

Although the UK has some of the most robust preventative counter-terrorism laws and powers afforded to law enforcement in the world, including Ecomms surveillance, on 15 March 2019, two mosques in Christchurch were attacked and livestreamed by a white supremacist Brenton Tarrant, resulting in 51 deaths and 40 injuries.[484] The attacks were live streamed through

---

[484] E. A. Roy, H. Sherwood & N. Perveen, 'Christchurch attack: Suspect had white-supremacist symbols on weapons', The Guardian, 15 March 2019, at

social media and the recordings were still available online to view some six-months later. Following on from the two terrorist attacks in Christchurch, the heads of state Jacinda Ardern of New Zealand, and French President Emmanuel Macron, gathered together other heads of state and technology industry leaders to consider how to prevent online services from being used to disseminate terrorist and violent extremist content.[485] The nine-step guide was resulted, addressing such abuse of legitimate 21st Century technology.[486] Such steps include collective action, such as sharing technology development and facilitating machine learning and AI insights, and individual actions, such as improving the detection and removal of materials.[487]

---

https://www.theguardian.com/world/2019/mar/15/christchurch-shooting-new-zealand-suspect-white-supremacist-symbols-weapons (last visited 12 April 2023).

[485] P. Bishop & S. Macdonald, 'Terrorist Content and the Social Media Ecosystem: The Role of Regulation'. In F. Marone 'Digital Jihad: Online Communication and Violent Extremism'. Ledizioni LediPublishing, Italy, November 2019.

[486] Global Internet Forum to Counter Terrorism GIFCT, 'Actions to Address the Abuse of Technology to Spread Terrorist and Violent Extremist Content', 15 May 2019 at https://gifct.org/2019/05/15/actions-to-address-the-abuse-of-technology-to-spread-terrorist-and-violent-extremist-content/ (last visited 12 April 2023).

[487] *Ibid.*

Several new laws have been proposed and created before the Christchurch attack. Germany in 2017 passed the Network Enforcement Act (NetzDG) which requires platforms to remove or block illegal content within 24 hours. It includes fines of up to €50 million for systematic breaches.[488] In 2018 the European Commission's Regulation on preventing the dissemination of terrorist content online.[489] Following this and the Christchurch attack, in May 2020 the French National Assembly passed the Bill on countering online hate speech, known more commonly as the Avia Law. Similar to Germany, the law requires the removal of content within 24 hours and includes child sex abuse content and addition to terrorist related materials. Since its adoption, Avia received a large amount of criticism for controversially impeding on the freedom of expression.[490] Then on 18 June 2020, the

---

[488] See s. 4(2) of NetzDG and s. 30(2) of the Act on Regulatory Offences.

[489] European Union, European Commission, 'Proposal for a regulation of the European Parliament and of the Council on preventing the dissemination of terrorist content online', 2018/0331 (COD), 2018.

[490] Article 19, 'France: The online hate speech Law is a serious setback for freedom of expression', 15 June 2020, at https://www.article19.org/resources/france-the-online-hate-

Constitutional Court ruled the legal provisions 'infringe upon the exercise of freedom of expression and communication in a way that is not necessary, suitable and proportionate'.[491]

The UK had been working on the Online Harms white paper since April 2019, culminating three years into the Online Safety Act 2023.[492] The Act has twelve parts and fourteen schedules, and usefully provides some key definitions and interpretation for the UK courts to follow, on some rather trickly technological language, such as 'content', 'encounter', 'search service' and 'user-to-user service.' The Act is arranged to provide the regulator Ofcom (The Office of Communications) with increased powers to fine user-to-user services and other internet

---

speech-law-is-a-serious-setback-for-freedom-of-expression/ (last visited 12 January 2024).

[491] French Constitutional Court, 'Decision n2020-801 DC du 18 Juin 2020, Communiqué de presse', at https://www.conseil-constitutionnel.fr/actualites/communique/decision-n-2020-801-dc-du-18-juin-2020-communique-de-presse (last visited 12 January 2024).

[492] HM Government, Parliamentary Bills, Online Safety Bill, at https://bills.parliament.uk/bills/3137 (last visited 12 January 2024).

service companies who fail to comply with requests.[493] Ofcom are to fashion codes of practice for the duties imposed on user-to-user services and regulated search services.[494] The bulk of the Act imposes a duty of care on providers to carry out risk assessments and remove illegal content, with a specific Chapter protecting children.[495] This duty of care requires online platforms to have "robust and proportionate measures to deal with harms that could cause significant physical or psychological harm…such as misinformation and disinformation…".[496] The duty of care is of course, aimed at protecting all users from harmful and illegal content, whereby Part Ten of the Act introduces communication offences, criminalising harmful, false, and threatening communications, including

---

[493] For further details on Ofcom please visit https://www.ofcom.org.uk/home (last visited 13 January 2024).

[494] See the Online Safety Act 2023, Parts 2-9, 11 and 12.

[495] Online Safety Act 2023 s1(3). See also HM Government, Parliamentary Bills, Online Safety Bill, at https://bills.parliament.uk/bills/3137 (last visited 12 January 2024). See Online Safety Act 2023, Chapter 1-3 for Ofcom and Duty of Care, and Part 4 for the protection of children.

[496] Online Safety Act 2023 Part 3. See also HM Government, Policy Paper, Online Safety Bill: factsheet, at https://www.gov.uk/government/publications/online-safety-bill-supporting-documents/online-safety-bill-factsheet (last visited 12 January 2024).

photographic or film.[497] So, where does extremist and
terrorist material fall?

Extremist communication is not specifically covered,
so would naturally fall within the duty of care placed on
providers to prevent harmful content. [498] The largest issue
here is that the phrase *harmful* is not defined, and some
content viewed as extreme by the UK Government, might
not have the same public reaction. Extinction Rebellion
represents such a group, which the UK Government listed
alongside Islamist and far-right extremism and terrorism,
as posing a threat to UK democracy.[499] Concerningly, the
guidance explained that to look out for people who speak
strongly or emotionally about environmental issues like
climate change, ecology, species extinction, fracking,
airport expansion or pollution'.[500] The non-violent group
openly advocate for civil disobedience, as opposed to

---

[497] Online Safety Act.

[498] Online Safety Act.

[499] V. Dodd & J. Grierson, 'Terrorism police list
Extinction Rebellion as extremist ideology', 10 January 2020, at
https://www.theguardian.com/uk-news/2020/jan/10/xr-extinction-
rebellion-listed-extremist-ideology-police-prevent-scheme-
guidance (last visited 12 January 2024).

[500] *Ibid.*

focusing on the more traditional systems such as organised protests, petitions and writing to UK Members of Parliament.[501] This evidences that the UK Government has yet to legally define extremism, rendering the term entirely political in ascription.

User-to-user services will be under a duty of care to mitigate and manage the risk of harm to individuals, identified in recent illegal content risk assessment of the service. The idea behind section 9 is to prevent individuals from encountering priority illegal content by means of the service and to minimise the length of time for which any priority illegal content is present.[502]

Definitional Challenges

Harmful, like *extremism*, is subjective and depends on one's point of view. Elon Musk raised this issue during an interview with the BBC on 12 April 2023, when asked about his duty of care to remove harmful content and

---

[501] See Extinction Rebellion at https://extinctionrebellion.uk/the-truth/about-us/ (last visited 12 January 2024).

[502] See also Online Safety Act 2023 s59.

misinformation.[503] Musk expressed concern at the subjectivity of both terms of use and advocated for safeguarding freedom of expression and speech. He went on to say that '…free speech is meaningless if you don't allow people you don't like to say things you don't like…otherwise it's irrelevant and once you lose it [free speech] it doesn't come back.'[504] Misinformation and disinformation are likewise problematic phrases, because there is no universal arbitrator of such subjective terms. When describing hateful content to Musk, the reporter defined this as content that solicits a reaction, that might perhaps be 'slightly sexist or slightly racist'.[505] This was challenged by Musk stating that in light of the absence of an arbitrator, who is to say a person should be banned or removed from the social media platform for expressing such views.[506] Without clear legal definitions of such terms, it is clear to see that there will always be borderline

---

[503] J. Clayton, 'Elon Musk BBC interview: Twitter boss on layoffs, misinfo and sleeping in the office', BBC News, 12 April 2023 at https://www.bbc.co.uk/news/business-65248196 (last visited 13 January 2024).
[504] *Ibid.*
[505] *Ibid.*
[506] *Ibid.*

cases resulting in the removal of a person's freedom to express themselves online.

As with the case study above, some vulnerable children and young people are radicalised through online gaming chat functions. The Act only mentions direct messages sent by way of interaction through gaming once, as part of functionality within user-to-user services. The Act does provide some potential optionality should someone be expressing a harmful view, with being able to likewise express a view on the content including applying a "like" or "dislike" button or other button of that nature, or applying an emoji or symbol of any kind. However, this relies on the person effected, or those with access to the communication, reporting this to the user-to-user service. As in the case study example, this might not have happened, and he could have continued on his path of radicalisation.

This Act was criticized for embodying fuzzy distinctions between illegal and unwanted content. The legislation originally required tech platforms to moderate what it called 'legal but harmful' content, but this language was removed. It remains the case, however, that the Act drastically expands the powers of the UK Government to moderate online platforms. The UK's Open Rights Group has argued that the Act could damage freedom of expression, with platforms over-censoring to avoid legal liability.[507] This is supported by a report by the Centre for Democracy and Technology in the US suggests that the Act's lack of definitive definitions could lead to confusion and inconsistency in its enforcement, potentially harming freedom of expression.[508] Carnegie UK Trust on the other hand argue that the Act proposes to increase transparency, accountability, and user participation helping to mitigate concerns about censorship and protect freedom of expression.[509]

---

[507] Open Rights Group, 'Don't scan me! The 'spy clause' in the Online Safety Bill will outsource surveillance to private messaging apps', at https://www.openrightsgroup.org/campaign/save-encryption/ (last visited 14 January 2024).

[508] Centre for Democracy and Technology at https://cdt.org/ (last visited 14 January 2024).

[509] Collective Wellbeing Carnegie UK, 'Online Safety Bill: Second Reading Briefing Note', at https://d1ssu070pg2v9i.cloudfront.net/pex/pex_carnegie2021/2022/05/12103808/20220330-OSB-2R-summary-briefing-FINAL.pdf (last visited 14 January 2024).

Rather helpfully, terrorism on the other had does have a national legal definition for the Act to rely on, with s59 dealing specifically with illegal content, including terrorist material. This is defined in Schedule 5 as relying on the Terrorism Act 2000, the Anti-Terrorism, Crime and Security Act 2001, the Terrorism Act 2006 and inchoate offences. In relying on the current counter-terrorism legal structures, it provides some structural surety from s1 Terrorism Act 2000, and ss1-3 Terrorism Act 2006 that criminalises the encouragement and dissemination of terrorist publications.[510]

The word terrorism is mentioned more than a few times in the Act, providing a duty of care on providers of user-to-user services, to include in the terms of use how individuals are to be protected from terrorist content. Ofcom must prepare and issue a code of practice to this regard regarding terrorism content.[511] Interestingly, the Secretary of State is provided discretionary powers to modify the code of practice submitted in line with national

---

[510] Online Safety Act 2023, Schedule 5.
[511] Online Safety Act 2023, Schedule 4, 12 and 13.

security or public safety concerns.[512] A similar power operated for the review of the codes of practice.[513] This essentially provides increased governmental control, through Ofcom, onto user-to-user services and providers. Through the medium, the UK Government can exclude terrorist organisations and those supporting them, from having an online presence.

The question remains however, will these measures when introduced be adequate in protecting people from being drawn into extremism or terrorism? There is much emphasis on Ofcom and the codes of practice it must produce, without which the technology companies and user-to-user service providers would be left much more in the dark. The main contention here is the global nature of the Internet and the lack of international consensus on a legal definition of terrorism, which means that companies will have to decide which national definitions used to criminalise terrorism to follow. Remaining within this ambit, contention surrounds the fact that there is no one-size-fits-all all measure, given the diverse range of online

---

[512] Online Safety Act 2023, s44.
[513] *Ibid.*

illegal activity surrounding the many denotations of terrorism and extremism. With no internationally agreed definition of terrorism or extremism, and no international or national legal definition of extremism, the risk assessments are thereby left to the user-to-user provider and search service to implement and for Ofcom to enforce. On the one hand content could be removed that is legitimately dangerous, and on the other hand content could be removed that is not dangerous but rather thought-provoking. Borderline cases are bound to bring challenges and an erosion of the freedom of expression, protected by way of Article 10 European Convention on Human Rights, which is why laws of this nature have failed in other nation states.

The Online Safety Act offers further contention due to the fact it is widely understood to contain a mandate for client-side scanning, but it does not say so specifically. Client-side scanning is a technology for moderating content on encrypted messaging services. It involves software that resides on a user's smart device, and checks images being uploaded for matches against a database of prohibited content. The database does not contain the actual images, but instead has what are known as "neural hashes" – rather like digital fingerprints – that enable two images to be compared. The technology appears to be similar to that used for QR codes. Where there is a match, the system will take a pre-programmed action to remove or report it to the authorities. Although the technology is lagging behind, this power is encapsulated the authorisation provided to Ofcom to demand decryption of communications. Rather covertly placed under s121, Ofcom can serve a notice on user-to-user services to use accredited technology to identify terrorist or child sexual exploitation and abuse content, whether communicated publicly or *privately*. This notice can also include the identification of search content. Companies, such as Meta and Telegram objected to the provisions within the Online Safety Act that requires companies to use 'accredited technology' to scan users' messages for child sexual abuse, and other harmful materials. The Act does not say how these scans would be implemented, but IT and security experts say they are impossible to introduce without breaking end-to-end encryption.

Secondary Legislation: Reduction in Parliamentary Scrutiny

The passing of the Online Safety Act 2023 has fashioned unresolved challenges. The Act provides for a large amount of secondary legislation to be created, along with Ofcom's yet to be decided codes and guidance. This in turn has resulted in an unclear regulatory scope, as no one will know the totality of the measures implemented nor the potential full impact of the Act. Concerns remain regarding the role of the Secretary of State and Internet companies will simply not know where they fall within any definitional thresholds until this decision is made.[514] Adding further concerns is the fact that Parliamentary debate focused on the theoretical rather than practical application and central issues surrounding 'harms' remains without structured categories providing clarity. Section 28 provides children's risk assessment duties regarding potential harms. the Secretary of State can define these harms and instruct Ofcom to publish reports. The reports are to be created every three years, including information

---

[514] Online Safety Act 2023 s44.

on what content it deems harmful to children and adults on user-to-user services and content that is harmful to children on search services. Instead of setting out a clear legal definition of what is harmful, besides relying on adverse physical or psychological harm, the Act instead sets out a large amount of provisions based on assessing risk and potential harms to relevant age groups. This point was raised in the House of Lords' second reading, suggesting the Government list priority harms into the law, rather than relying on secondary legislation.[515]

Conclusion

Terrorist groups and self-starters have embraced modern communication technology, from marketing to coordinating an attack. Given these technological advancements have brought about economic and societal change, it is of little surprise that it has had a similar effect of terrorism and criminality. It is interesting to note that in response the then UK Prime Minister David Cameron

---

[515] See https://d1ssu070pg2v9i.cloudfront.net/pex/pex_carnegie2021/2022/05/12103808/20220330-OSB-2R-summary-briefing-FINAL.pdf p7 (last visited 28 January 2024).

announced that if he was leading the next government, he would introduce legislation in 2016 to eliminate 'safe spaces' for terrorists to communicate. Clearly this has failed to come to fruition.

It is estimated that technology doubles every two years. Although beyond the ambit of this book, this figure is now vehemently contested with some recent debates suggesting technological advancements are slowing down. However, for Tim Simonite's growth in mobile telephonic smart phone applications, the figure of two years could be a little low. It is reasonably well known the legislature is slow in keeping up with the growth in technology, and it is surmised this would continue for the foreseeable future. A unique threat has been created, whereby the vertical effects of terrorist groups' communication radicalise others, then the horizontal effect that allows people to operate under an anonymity cloak, who have advanced independent operational abilities with potential access to explosives and firearms purchased on the darknet.

Considering this predicament, legislation, namely the IPA, has been created aimed at policing the Internet. A cooperative approach with ISP's is essential to this aim, ensuring the dark sides of the web are monitored and then removed should they be deemed illegal. It is also essential the Government collaborate with smart phone application providers to allow targeted decryption of messages.

The freedom of expression is simply that. The express yourself and share your beliefs freely without fear of persecution. It is an inherent and essential part of democracy. The government and political parties encourage citizens to be more politically active, but being radical or having dissenting views is not. So, where do we draw the line? The commissioning or committing of a criminal offence or civil tort appears to be a natural place to draw the solid red line. The recommended standard is good, strong legislation that holds within it precise and definitive definitions. Providing the UK courts with an objective test is another.

With an increasingly authoritarian government and increased security governance regarding policing the risk society in the UK, we are certainly seeing further containments placed around the freedom of expression and civil liberties. The increase in secondary legislation and use of Henry VIII Clauses, coupled with the lack of legal definitional certainty of phrases, fashions an unpredictable future regarding online functionality. One might suggest that rather than legalising and regulating the Internet, which is the intent, it is in fact being politicised. The government of the day can decide what is extreme, what is radical and what is harmful. Utilising the bulk surveillance powers of collection, retention and equipment interference under IPA, this new Online Safety Act 2023 plugs the gaps in controlling what is said and shared on the Internet. The Online Safety Act 2023 is by all accounts a grand attempt to grasp by the horns so to speak, illegal content and terrorist/extremist activity by regulating internet platforms. However, as noted by Lord Anderson in his 2023 report 'such laws are no substitute for covert investigatory powers, used to detect and counter the threats to UK individuals.'[516]

One must recall that being radical and extreme on the one hand can bring about positive change, such as the

---

[516] Supra as per Lord David Anderson, https://assets.publishing.service.gov.uk/government/uploads/system/uploads/attachment_data/file/1166726/Independent_Review_of_the_Investigatory_Powers_Act_2016-FINAL.pdf accessed 20 February 2024.

advocation for and creation of the UK's Constitutional Monarchy, the independence gained by many countries once in the British Empire, and even the Suffragettes. Change that of course has since been celebrated. For this reason, we must have laws that precisely criminalise certain behaviour, protect the vulnerable and promote legal fairness and freedoms. Rather than political censorship and exerting too much control over dissenting ideals.

WOMAN SUFFRAGE
1920-1970
RIGHT TO VOTE
VOTES FOR WOMEN
50TH ANNIVERSARY
U.S. 6¢

About the Author

Dr. Simon Hale-Ross is a Senior Lecturer in Law and an expert in counterterrorism law and policy. His expertise is broadly Public Law, including terrorism, serious organized crime, internet law and human rights. He is a Senior Fellow of the Higher Education Academy, an award-winning senior lecturer and known for his learning and teaching excellence.

Milton Keynes UK
Ingram Content Group UK Ltd.
UKHW020256200624
444124UK00002BA/13

9 781917 306331